I0488225

Conundrum

Conundrum

The Challenge of Execution in Middle-Market Companies

Lawrence J. Kendzior

iUniverse, Inc.
New York Lincoln Shanghai

Conundrum
The Challenge of Execution in Middle-Market Companies

All Rights Reserved © 2004 by Lawrence J. Kendzior

No part of this book may be reproduced or transmitted in any form or by any means, graphic, electronic, or mechanical, including photocopying, recording, taping, or by any information storage retrieval system, without the written permission of the publisher.

iUniverse, Inc.

For information address:
iUniverse, Inc.
2021 Pine Lake Road, Suite 100
Lincoln, NE 68512
www.iuniverse.com

ISBN: 0-595-30985-2

Printed in the United States of America

This is dedicated to the many business owners, clients and friends alike, who have laid the foundation for my education in the concepts discussed in this book.

A special thanks goes to those clients, friends and associates who read, discussed, and provided constructive thoughts and ideas throughout the development of this work.

CONTENTS

HOW TO READ <u>CONUNDRUM</u>

I wrote this book in the middle of a busy professional consulting career—in between working with clients, waiting for business associates in meeting rooms and airports, and while otherwise dealing with the exigencies of a fast-paced professional life. The resulting keen appreciation of the need for saving time through the use of focus and discipline has therefore been incorporated in the book from the beginning.

This is a "multi-level" work, developed in a manner that saves time for busy owners and business people, and that is entertaining as well.

Before starting your read, flip through the entire book, reading the bold face type in the text boxes. If these main points interest you, go ahead and read the first 172 pages. Since many business theory books, even those that are perfectly valid, can get boring, I've wrapped an entertaining little novel around the meat of the material. Kind of like the rice you find around the fish you find in sushi.

Then, if you find that you'd like to try the concepts in this book, go to the supplementary material in the back of the book for the tools you'll need to implement these concepts in your own company. Kind of like the seaweed wrapper you find around the rice in sushi.

Finally, if you'd like to jump-start the entire process of improving your company, go to the web site at **www.conundrumonline.com**. Check out the case studies of companies who have successfully used the principles in this book. Then, evaluate your company, identify its key issues, and start the action steps necessary to resolve them—TODAY.

This last part doesn't have anything to do with sushi!

PREFACE

Although this book is in novel format, the principles it embodies and the examples used as illustrations are real. They are drawn from real life experiences with organizations of all sizes over the last 30-plus years. The term "organizations" rather than "companies" is used here because many of the principles of leadership, organization and discipline you'll find in this book were drawn from early military experience—rifle teams, squads, platoons, and infantry rifle companies. Many of the lessons learned from military organizations are directly applicable to parallel commercial organizations—teams, departments, work groups—and manufacturing, distribution, or service companies.

Those of us who have been in business awhile realize that all companies have business plans, written or otherwise. But many companies experience difficulty in bringing their plans to fruition. As a business consultant, much of my early career was spent in trying to help companies fix problems caused by the inability to execute. But in those days, I rarely recognized the problem as such.

After a number of years of sometimes getting results, sometimes not, I discovered an important principle: A small amount of business planning well executed is worth much more than a thick volume of business plans poorly executed. Also, many if not most companies fail not because of bad planning, but because of bad (or no) execution. It was also interesting to note that a large percentage of my clients in trouble seemed to fall into the "late Phase II" category on the growth curve (see *Exhibit A* at the back of this book). This phenomenon taught the lesson that, although some companies can grow to a certain size based upon the sheer talent, sales ability, or force of will of the owner, good execution beyond a certain point on the company's growth curve requires infrastructure—appropriate management, systems, and planning. It is this infrastructure that develops the focus and discipline necessary for good execution.

I soon discovered, however, that learning the above was not enough. Even though I had learned what separated good companies from the not so good, I still needed a system that could help my clients build the infrastructure they required to execute their business plans. That's where I ran into this **Conundrum**—*If a* *company needs infrastructure in order to execute, how can it execute the actions it needs to take in order to build infrastructure in the first place?* The experiences of my colleagues and myself eventually evolved the answer. My firm and clients have used the Issue/Action Agenda (see *Exhibit E* at the back of this book) and related system for several years now in obtaining superior results. Unlike many "consulting systems," our system is 10 % planning and 90 % execution—and has proven to be a very successful formula in helping our client companies **achieve** what they **plan**.

My hope for this book is that it will help your company do the same.

Larry Kendzior
December 2003

Chapter 1

Jerry was having a six thirty am breakfast at the O'Hare Marriott in Chicago. Later that day, he would be presenting a proposal to a major electronic original equipment manufacturer (OEM) on behalf of his company, a tier two component supplier. The potential five million dollar order, with the probability of recurring add-on business should have meant a lot to Jerry's $22 million company, Cleveland Electronics.

Yet, Jerry wasn't a happy man. As he sat contemplating whether to go with the breakfast buffet or a bagel and cream cheese, he couldn't suppress a feeling of impending doom. What's going on? Was he afraid he wouldn't get the order? He pondered this as he ordered the buffet.

"Why am I afraid?" he thought. *"If they don't give me the order, all we've lost is time—and a $600 airfare back to Cleveland."*

Jerry thought about a discussion he had had with Dave Kork, his controller, just last afternoon. They were going over the company's financial affairs, and both Jerry and Dave were puzzled.

Jerry—"I don't understand it. Sales are up for the third year in a row. But our suppliers are screaming and the bank's wondering why we're asking for another increase in the credit line. What gives, Dave?"

Dave—"Well, one answer is that even though sales are up, our profits are down."

Jerry—"Why?"

Dave—"Can't really tell, other than our costs are up across the board."

Jerry—"But we made money last year, and the year before that. Why is it that we seem to have hit the brick wall?"

Dave—"I can't really tell. Shall I call the managers together and see if we can come up with an answer?"

Jerry—"No, we don't have time for that, I've got the presentation to Unisonictelcom in Chicago tomorrow, and I need Stan and the boys to finish up their pieces of the presentation for me."

Dave—"Well, I'll try to do some more analysis over the weekend, and we can talk more about it when you get back."

Jerry—"Yeah. It'd be nice to figure out why we're losing ten cents with every new dollar of sales we bring into the place."

Suddenly, another thought flashed through Jerry's mind—*"That's it! That's why I'm feeling this impending doom! It's not because of fear we won't get the order-it's fear we **will** get the order. Let's see, a ten-percent loss on five million dollars of sales. That's a good start down the bankruptcy trail. No wonder I've lost my appetite."*

With that, Jerry paid the breakfast tab and returned to his room to get ready for the big proposal.

Chapter 2

Chicago's O'Hare airport, 2:00 PM.

Jerry's reading the day's **Wall Street Journal** while waiting for his flight back to Cleveland. The financial news is good; his prospect, the electronics OEM, reports sales and profits for the next quarter are expected to be up by six percent.

The presentation to the prospect went well. At lunch, Jerry was told that his chances of getting the five million dollar order were "better than 50/50."

And Jerry's having a hard time focusing on the financial news. Breakfast's nagging feeling in the pit of his stomach is still with him. *What if we get the order…and lose even more money than we would have without the darn thing?"* Jerry thought.

Just then, his cell phone went off. It was Jacqueline, his 14-year-old daughter.

"Hi, sweetie…how's everything?" Jerry asked.

"Oh, just fine, Dad, but…" his daughter's voice tails off.

"But what, honey?"

"Well, its just that Mom told me before she left for the store an hour ago that she and I are moving out of the house this afternoon," she said.

"Whaaaat…" exclaimed Jerry. He felt like a 300 lb. Cleveland Brown left tackle had just dropped off of a five-story office building and landed smack dab in the middle of his chest.

"Yeah, Dad, she said she's had enough of your late nights, out of town travel, and your not being here mentally even when you are home," said Jacqueline.

"Put your mother on the phone," said Jerry.

"Can't, Dad. She's not back from the store yet."

"Well…well…have her call me the minute she gets back."

"OK, yeah, sure," said Jacqueline. "By the way, Dad, do you have your special watch on? The one that has the day and date?"

Jerry thought, *"What in the hell does she care about what day it is, for crying out loud?"*

"Yes sweetie," said Jerry.

"Well, daddy, what day is it?"

"Honey, its Tuesday, April 1, if that makes any difference," said Jerry.

Oh, oh. Jerry was starting to get it. Flashback to a year ago. He and wife Gina had really set Jacqueline up for a great April Fool piece of fun. After they'd sprung it on their 13-year-old, the kid had laughed up a storm—and then swore she'd get back at them.

"Jacqueline, honey…you wouldn't be trying to fool your loving father, now would you?" questioned Jerry.

"April Fool, Dad." his loving daughter replied.

"Ha Ha. Now tell Mom I'm in the coronary emergency unit of Chicago's Resurrection Hospital, and tell her to come to the phone right away."

"Sorry, Dad, I've had enough April fooling for one day," said Jacqueline.

"Then just ask her to come to the phone."

Jacqueline put her Mom on.

"Hi, darling. How'd the big meeting go today?" asked Gina, Jerry's wife.

"Well, honey, the meeting went well, but I can't shake this feeling of impending doom—except for just now, when your kid just about gave me a coronary."

"What's that all about?" asked Gina.

Jerry spent the next few minutes relating his feelings at breakfast, the meeting, and Jacqueline's April fool trick.

Gina said, "Well, it sounds like you've had quite a day. Tell you what. When you get to Cleveland, why don't you take a cab to the airport hotel? I'll meet you there. We'll have ourselves a little welcome home treat, and do dinner before you come home tonight."

"That sounds great, honey. Will you make the reservations?" asked Jerry.

"Yes. See you at the airport hotel around six thirty?" asked Gina.

"See you then, sweetheart. I can't wait." Jerry pushed END on his cell phone and boarded the plane.

Chapter 3

9:30 PM. that same day. Jerry and Gina are enjoying an after-dinner coffee at the airport hotel.

"Well," remarked Jerry, "the last part of my day was definitely more...uh...stimulating than the first part."

"Really," said Gina. "Which part of the last part did you find most stimulating?"

"I thought the part where you took my part in between your parts and then you..."

"Honey," said Gina, "you'd better stop now or we're going to end up going back to the room—and we can't leave the kid alone for much longer."

"I agree." said Jerry. "What do you think about that feeling of fear I told you I felt at breakfast?" Jerry had described his premonition to Gina between breaks in the hotel room.

"From what you've said tonight and in little snatches over the past few weeks, I don't think your premonition is unfounded. I only wish I had majored in business instead of English lit. Maybe then I'd be better equipped to help you out," said Gina.

"Yeah, but just your objective input is valuable. What do you think I should do about it?" asked Jerry.

Gina remembered a dinner conversation she and Jerry had with their close friends Bruce and Lynn a few weeks ago. Bruce owned a successful 100-employee company that had fallen on hard times several years ago. He had been very successful in turning the company around, and now his 300-employee company was, according to Bruce and Lynn, both "highly profitable" and "running like a top."

Gina said, "Do you remember Bruce and Lynn talking about the success they've enjoyed with Bruce's company?"

"Yes, but what's that got to do with me?" asked Jerry. "Bruce builds plastic injection molds. He's a job shop. We manufacture electronic components."

"Jerry, remember what Bruce was saying about how he turned the company around—something about using his accountant?"

"Yeah—you know, Gina, you're right," said Jerry. "Except, I don't think he said he used his accountant. What he said was he thought his accountant was the one who helped him get into trouble in the first place."

Gina replied, "Why don't you call Bruce tomorrow and ask him about it?"

"Good idea, sweetie. Ready to go home and beat the kid?"

"I took care of that before we met at the hotel," Gina replied sweetly.

Chapter 4

Bruce and Jerry went 'way back. Bruce, five years older than Jerry, was a struggling 32-year-old mold maker when he started his own company. He borrowed $15,000 against his house and rented 150 square feet of space from a machine shop in a suburban Cleveland industrial park. Jerry was a rising star sales representative for a large electronics firm. He met Bruce through a neighbor, the banker to whom Bruce had turned to get his $15,000 of start-up capital. A casual conversation in Jerry's driveway led to a Saturday-night get together with the wives, a few games of golf, and the rest was history. Jerry and Bruce became fast friends in spite of their personality differences. Fast friends because they shared an interest in golf and business. Different because, although both men loved to have fun and could regale each other with hilarious jokes and tall tales, Bruce was detail oriented, methodical, and, when it came to business, a real strategic thinker.

Jerry, on the other hand, tended toward the big picture. His personality was bubbling and frequently charming. He preferred to use these traits to sell himself, his position, his ideas and his company. Details, although necessary and important, were best left to someone else for follow up.

"Morning Bruce," said Jerry from his office phone at 10: 30 the next morning. "How are things in the world of plastics?"

Bruce replied, "Great so far Jer. It's early enough so that things really haven't had a chance to fall apart yet. Listen, I've got a meeting ready to start in a couple of minutes, and I need to get some things ready. Can I call you back this afternoon?"

"I just have a quickie, Bruce. What's the name of that accountant or consultant or…whatever…you mentioned at dinner the week before last?"

Bruce replied, "A quickie? Ordinarily, Jerry, I wouldn't let that one get by. But, I've got to get going. The fellow's name is Mike Henderson and his number is (216) 555-1254."

"Thanks, Bruce."

"Jerry, I'll call you later this afternoon."

Five hours later, Bruce called Jerry from the golf course.

"Well, Jerry, did you get ahold of Henderson yet?"

"No, I haven't had the time. All kinds of happy hell's broken loose around here," said Jerry. "Bruce, remember that five million order dollar I was telling you about?"

"How could I forget? You were so excited about it you almost choked on your pasta at dinner," said Bruce. "And that's a real trick. One I've only seen done at old peoples' homes," needled Bruce.

"Yeah, well, Unisonictelcom called two hours ago. We got the order," said Jerry.

"I ley, that's great, buddy. No wonder you haven't had time to call Henderson. He's a great fellow. But, as I think I mentioned, he's a little weird."

"Wasn't he your accountant or something?" asked Jerry.

"No, said Bruce. I think he had an accounting degree, but back when I met him, he'd been working as a consultant to owner-managed companies. For about 20 years at that time, I think. Why'd you ask for his name?"

Jerry related the story from the night before, and his fears about the big order causing him to lose even more money. Bruce related how that sounded a lot like a situation he himself had gotten into with his company in the past.

"But Jerry," said Bruce, "when I got into my fix, the numbers were a lot smaller than the ones you're talking about today."

Jerry said, "I'll give your Mr. Henderson a call tomorrow. I have to spend the rest of today and tonight making sure we've got the customer's specs right and that the suppliers are lined up."

"Don't wait too long," said Bruce as he signed off.

Chapter 5

A couple of weeks later.

Jerry and his controller Dave are locked in tense conversation. The bank just called. Yesterday, checks started bouncing, and today was payday. No money had been deposited in the corporate coffers in the last two days.

"Dave," Jerry asked tersely, "why the hell isn't there any money in our accounts?"

"I don't really know," said Dave, "but I can take a guess. The books haven't been balanced in a while because I've had the accounting department busy working on the big order. And anyway, we've still got two point eight million dollars available on the credit line, so it's no big deal."

"No big deal?" Jerry asked. His voice had just gone from terse and low to definitely on the rise—to match his temper. "No big deal that we don't even know how much money we've got? And I'm supposed to tell that to Rich and Tony over at the Bank?"

"You can't tell them that," said Dave. "Give me a half hour to work up a plausible story, and let me give them a call myself."

"OK, but run the explanation by me first."

"Right, Jerry. And it won't happen again," Dave said with an apologetic tone in his voice.

Jerry only said, "Please shut the door on your way out."

After the door closed, Jerry's mind went wild. This wasn't the first time in the past two years that something like this had happened. And, these unpleasant surprises weren't only coming from Accounting. Jerry started thinking, *"Now what would Bruce do..."* when he remembered that he'd never called Henderson after the last time that he and Bruce spoke.

"My God," exclaimed Jerry out loud, "it's been over two weeks."

With that, Jerry went through the stack of yellow stickies piling up on the side of his telephone. Luckily, he found the sticky labeled *Mike Henderson*, and could just barely make out the last two digits of Henderson's phone number. This was a fortunate circumstance, since the sticky had gone home with him the day Jerry wrote down Henderson's number. At desert that night, Jerry had spilled hot fudge Sundae over the note as he discussed it with his wife Gina. The next morning, the sticky made its way back to his office where it joined the other 50 million little yellow notes stacked up by Jerry's phone.

Jerry dialed the number. Luckily, he got through to Henderson immediately. After 15 or 20 minutes of probing discussion, Mike asked Jerry, "Do you fish?"

"Huh?" replied Jerry. They had been discussing the people on Cleveland Electronics' management team. Fish was about as far away as one could get from the gist of the conversation they'd been having. "Did you say 'fish'?"

"Yes," said Mike. "As in grouper, yellowtail, sailfish, bonefish."

"Why'd you ask that?" said Jerry, his face screwed up so tight it looked like a wet washcloth being wrung out by the 300-pound Cleveland Brown tackle.

"Well, Jerry, I think I know what may be wrong at your company. Problem is, it's a serious situation, it will take some time to look at some facts to confirm my tentative diagnosis, and I'm on a flight to my place down in the Florida Keys in the morning."

"Oh, just super," Jerry remarked sarcastically. "Isn't there anything you can help me with right now? Can't we "Band-Aid" something over the phone that will hold me over until you get back?"

"Let me think a minute," said Mike.

The line went silent for a full half minute. Jerry, who as an amateur radio announcer in college had come to hate dead air like the plague, started a quick game of **Free Cell** on his computer. Finally, Mike spoke up.

"Why don't you grab a flight down to my place in the Keys tomorrow afternoon or the day after? By that time, I'll have had a chance to get a line wet, and then I'll be able to focus in on your problem a little bit better."

Jerry thought for a few seconds. "I can do that," he said, "but the airfare's going to cost me an arm and a leg."

Mike replied, "The airfare won't be as much as my fee, and the fee and airfare together will look like *chum change* compared to the money your company's losing every day we don't fix your problem."

"Excuse me, Mike," said Jerry. "You did say *chump change*, didn't you?

"No," replied Mike, "I said *chum change*. Like in fish bait. You spread *chum* in the water to bring the fish to your boat. See, mentally I'm already down there."

With that, Jerry and Mike worked out the details of the travel arrangements, wished each other an easy trip, talked about Mike's fees and billing arrangements, and hung up.

After another hour at the office, Jerry went home to pack.

Chapter 6

Two days later.

It was a hot August afternoon down in the Keys. Jerry and Mike were sitting in the shade on Mike's boat, tied to a dock behind Mike's small canal home. Jerry had just spent the last two hours telling the story of his company to Mike. They were now in the middle of talking about some of the hardships Jerry had gone through over the past couple of years.

"Jerry, it sounds like the company's had a tough time recently. Didn't you ever hit critical mass and make a lot of money?"

"It depends on what you mean by a lot of money," replied Jerry. "And yeah, about six or seven years after I started the company we were really hitting on all cylinders. I had four or five really good people working for me, and things were small enough that I really felt like I was in control. I closed on all the really big orders, and my people would follow up. During those times, we had no worries, and made a lot of money."

Mike then asked, "What's a lot of money, and how much were you selling with how many people?"

Jerry replied, "When things were going well, we were doing about nine million dollars in sales with around 60 to 70 people. If memory serves correctly, we were making a little over a million a year."

"That's really commendable," said Mike sincerely. "What happened?"

Jerry took a long pull of his Miller Lite, gave it a moment, and then said thoughtfully, "Well, we got bigger. Things got out of control. My best sales rep, whom I was grooming to take my place as head of sales, left to start his own company. We got bigger and bigger in terms of sales and people. But our bottom line has never again hit the million dollar mark."

"So what you're telling me," said Mike, "is that your sales have grown from nine million dollars to $22 million over the last 5 years?"

"Yep," said Jerry with a bottle draining pull on the Miller Lite.

"That's about a 20 % annual growth rate," said Mike.

"Uh huh."

"But your profits haven't grown. Hmmm…how much did your company make last year?"

"We'll…we do a lot of tax planning and other kinds of maneuvering now to minimize income taxes but still make the financial statements look good to the bank," said Jerry. "To tell you the truth, I don't really know how much we made last year."

"Here's my cell phone," replied Mike. "Call your controller and find out. Meantime, I'm going to clean some of the yellowtail I caught this morning."

A half-hour later, Jerry related that, after adjusting for all the tax saving maneuvering and window dressing, Cleveland Electronics and Manufacturing had made a little over $250,000 last year.

"So in short Jerry, sales zoomed **up** from nine million dollars to $22 million, but your profits shot **down** from one million dollars to $250,000?"

"That's about it. And to top it all off, the last year and a half at the company feels like a war's been going on. Employees bickering, customers complaining and their complaints going unresolved, cash flow shortages, bankers making like they'd like to call in my credit, the whole shot. Yeah, that's just about right. A real war."

> "…sales zoomed <u>up</u> from nine million dollars to $22 million, your profits shot <u>down</u> from one million dollars to $250,000?…"

"Jerry, were you ever in the military?" asked Mike.

"No, but…"

"Well, let me tell you something. Don't **even** try to compare business to the military," said Mike.

"Oh, really," said Jerry, a trifle sarcastically. "And why, pray tell, is that?"

"I was in the Army," said Mike. "Infantry branch—four years. Paying them back for my college education. And I can tell you, there's two *huge* differences between a bad day in the Army and a bad day at the office."

"And those would be?"

"Well, mused Mike, "the first thing I always remember when I'm having a bad day at the office is...

The bullets aren't real."

"Ha, ha" laughed Jerry. "And the second thing is...."

"Remember this the next time you or one of your office people make a really, really bad mistake:

When you screw up in business, nobody gets killed," laughed Mike.

"OK, Captain Comedy, that's swell," chuckled Jerry. "Now how about fixing my company before this sun and the beer fries our brains and we won't be able to think?"

"My pleasure, Lieutenant," said Mike. "Jerry, your description of your company's *feeling* like a war zone probably is very accurate. In fact, what we're going to cover while you're down here was discussed in an article written by Larry E. Greiner in the **Harvard Business Review**. He called the article 'Evolution and Revolution as Organizations Grow'[1], expounded Mike. "The point of the article, and a lot of work that was done before and after, is that companies go through several stages of growth. In fact, a mature company's entire life cycle can be diagrammed like this:

---

1 Larry E. Greiner, HARVARD BUSINESS REVIEW, May–June 1998

Evolution and revolution in Privately Held Companies

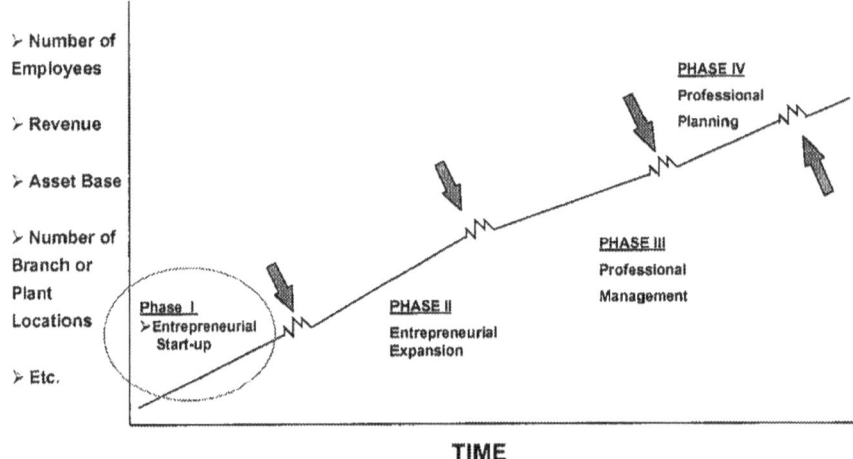

GROWTH INDICATORS

"Well, the revolution part certainly fits my company," agreed Jerry.

"The point of the article, and a lot of work that was done before and after, is that companies go through several stages of growth. In fact, a mature company's entire life cycle can be diagrammed like the graph shown above. Each of the Phases describe a stage in the life cycle of a company:

> Phase I is **start up**
>
> Phase II is **entrepreneurial expansion**
>
> Phase III is **professional management**
>
> Phase IV is **professional management and planning**"

"Interesting," said Jerry.

"Glad you think so," said Mike. "The thing that I as a consultant have to keep in mind is that a company's management practices and infrastructure change dramatically as it moves along the growth curve. Therefore, it's essential for consultants to be sure of where the client falls on the curve—because

> "...it's essential for consultants to be sure of where the client falls on the curve—because our recommendations will be different for a Phase II company than, say, a Phase III company."

our recommendations will be different for a Phase II company than, say, a Phase III company."

"Makes sense to me," said Jerry. "What are those squiggley lines between each phase?"

Mike explained, "Those squiggley lines are the revolution, Jerry. They represent crisis points the company experiences in trying to go from one phase to the next. Notice I said '*trying*'. Not all companies successfully make it to the next higher phase."

"I get your point," said Jerry. "So, its obvious to me that the reason my company feels like a war zone is that it's in the middle of one of these crisis points?"

"Maybe not in the <u>middle</u>," replied Mike.

"Well, how do I find out where we are and how to fix it?"

"Let's take it a step at a time," said Mike. "Do you like to fish, Jerry?"

"Not really."

"Shame. Well, I'll tell you what. The yellowtail bite is really hot down here right now, and I need to rig up for some night fishing. Why don't you clean up, have dinner in town, and get a good night's sleep. We'll pick up on this in the morning."

"Come on, Mike, we're just getting started. Why not just continue our talk through dinner?" asked a disappointed Jerry.

"Because you're not paying me enough to miss a couple of hours of hot yellowtail fishing. And, once you taste one of those fish at lunch tomorrow, you're going to wish you went with me."

"OK, you win. I'm going to clean up for dinner. Good luck tonight, Mike."

"Same to you, Jerry."

Chapter 7

8:00 AM the next morning. Mike and Jerry are having coffee on Mike's patio. Mike had just finished going over last evening's yellowtail catch "…32 really nice little scrappers, and I let another 30 or so go!" exclaimed Mike.

"So, how did **your** evening go, Jerry?"

"Not too badly, although I should have gone home after dinner."

"Went to the movies like you were talking about yesterday?" asked Mike.

"No. Interestingly enough, while I was having dinner, I got into a really interesting discussion with my waitress. A short, very thin, very tan lady. She came down to the Keys several years ago and started hanging around with Mel Fisher, the famous treasure hunter who discovered the $400 million payload on the **Atocha**. Since then, she's been doing her own little treasure dives on the reefs around here."

Mike replied, "You know, they're still finding odd bits of sunken Spanish ships, coins, and the like around the Keys. Especially after one of their hurricanes blows through and stirs up the sea bottom."

"Yep. In fact, she was saying that she had actually found a wonderful 1733 silver Cobb coin just last month. Showed it to me right there in the restaurant. We got to talking, and I thought it would make a swell gift for Gina's birthday which is coming up in a few months."

"Those coins make beautiful and interesting jewelry, you know," commented Mike.

"That's where I was last night," replied Jerry excitedly. "After talking to the waitress about her coin, I stopped in a couple of jewelry stores around town and priced some settings. It'll be an expensive present, but Gina would be thrilled. Imagine a 270-year-old coin as a pendant on a gold neck chain. Jewelry that's also a piece of history! I was so wound up when I got back to the hotel, I didn't fall asleep until 3:00 AM."

"No wonder yours eyes are a little red around the rims," said Mike. "Now let's get down to business."

"Fine by me," said Jerry, taking a sip of his coffee. "Can you expand on those four growth phases we were talking about last afternoon?"

"Absolutely," Mike declared. "In fact, to make it even clearer to you, I'll give you one of my presentations to take with you to read on the plane."

(Readers will find this presentation at Exhibit A in the back of this book).

"Great," said Jerry.

"OK, now the way I like to work with these four growth phases is to talk about each phase in terms of its

   —Characteristics
   —Problem areas
   —Crisis points and
   —Management emphasis,"

said Mike.

"Management emphasis of what?" queried Jerry.

"Management emphasis on issues that are needed to overcome each set of crisis points," said Mike.

"That makes sense to me," said Jerry, "but won't it take a lot of time to go through all of those steps for each phase?"

"It sure will," said Mike. "And from discussing your personality with your pal Bruce, I know that you've got the worst case of attention deficit he's ever seen in a young business owner."

"Well, at least he got the young part right," snapped Jerry.

"Excuse me, Jerry. What'd you say? I wasn't paying attention," Mike said over a short laugh.

"Yeah, right. At what I'm paying you an hour, the jokes better get better, is all I'm hoping for," said Jerry.

"OK, OK, so what we're going to do now is an overview. Then, you're going to take home the presentation and an evaluation tool. The evaluation tool, which you can work through on the plane ride home, will tell you what phase your company is in. That information and the presentation I gave you will point out the things we need to focus on in order to fix your company. Comprende?"

> "The evaluation tool... will tell you what phase your company is in. That information and the presentation I gave you will point out the things we need to focus on in order to fix your company..."

"I think so," answered Jerry. "How did you ever come across this... this...model?"

"Yeah, model's a good name," replied Mike. "In fact, because I use it to emphasize business strategy in working with my clients, I like to call it the Business Growth Model."

Mike continued, "As far as I can tell, the concept of these four growth phases evolved in the late 1970's when the venture capital guys were trying to figure out how to value companies they were considering investing money in. The idea was that the later a company's growth phase, the more the company was worth, all other things being equal."

"So," said Jerry, "I can actually increase the value of Cleveland Electronics by moving it farther along on the growth curve?"

"Exactly right," said Mike. "In fact, a while ago a Chicago-area accounting and consulting firm did some studies, and found these phase/multiple correlations:

Phase	Range of multiples
I	1.7 to 3.0
II	2.5 to 3.5
III	3.0 to 5.0
IV	4.0 to 6.0"

"Wow," said Jerry. "That's really something. So I increase the value of my company solely by working on moving it farther out on the growth curve?"

"Not really," said Mike.

"What do you mean by that?" asked Jerry, exasperated.

"First of all," said Mike, "understand that you used the word 'solely.' Although the Business Growth Model addresses a lot of things that impact value, it doesn't address them all."

> "Although the Business Growth Model addresses a lot of things that impact value, it doesn't address them all"

"What doesn't it address?"

"The biggest missing factor is the industry the company operates in and, in particular from a value standpoint, the growth rate of the industry relative to the growth rate of the company being valued," said Mike.

"What else?" asked Jerry.

"Another major factor is earnings," explained Mike. "While doing a lot of things suggested by the Business Growth Model will increase both the company's multiple and its earnings, the Model isn't all inclusive."

"You mean companies can make a lot of money without doing the things encompassed in the Business Growth Model?" asked Jerry.

"Of course they can," explained Mike. "However, most companies find it difficult to sustain profitability without doing much of the business planning and management infrastructure building suggested by the Model. And the sooner a company realizes what needs to be done and how to do it, the quicker the return to profitability," said Mike.

> "...most companies find it difficult to sustain profitability without doing much of the business planning and management infrastructure building suggested by the Model"

"And the less likely it is that the company will wind up in bankruptcy court?" asked Jerry.

"Exactly," Mike replied.

For the next couple of hours, Jerry and Mike went over the Model in more detail and discussed Jerry's company. Finally, Jerry said, "It's getting about time for me to leave for the airport. Where are we going from here?"

"Well, you're going to the airport, and I'm taking the boat to a little patch reef about 200 yards southeast of the Coffins Patch marker buoy. One of my favorite snapper spots" said Mike.

"Ha," snorted Jerry. "I meant, where do we go when it comes to fixing my company?"

Mike replied, "Oh. Well…like we discussed earlier, you'll complete the evaluation on the plane home. I'd have your managers complete it, too, and then compare results. When you have agreement as to the phase your company's in, give me a call and we'll do the next step together," said Mike.

"The next step will be the things we need to do to fix my company?" asked Jerry.

"Yes."

"Mike, can you tell me exactly how this Business Growth Model is going to fix things?" asked Jerry.

"Jerry, the main problems with your company have to do with planning and execution-the two main things a company has to do well in order to succeed on a long-term basis. Some name the model *Strategic Growth Model* because strategy helps a company develop focus. And, as you will see in a few weeks, the presentation I gave you contains action items to help you and your managers execute the key items needed to put Cleveland Electronics back on track. Now, will you please excuse me while I go buy some bait?" asked Mike.

> "…the main problems with your company have to do with planning and execution-the two main things a company has to do well in order to succeed on a long-term basis."

"Have a ball, Mike," replied Jerry.

Chapter 8

On the flight home, Jerry thought about some of the key points he and Mike had covered. He took a pad out of his briefcase and wrote the points down so he could review them with his management team tomorrow.

1) Companies can grow and prosper on the sales and technical talents of the owner/founder. But most companies will at some time "hit the wall."

2) "Hitting the wall" means that the company is encountering certain crisis points that are preventing it from going to the next level.

3) "Hitting the wall" usually shows up as flat sales or profits. But flat sales or profits are usually merely symptoms, not the cause of the company's core problems.

4) The approach to fixing a company in this situation is **not** to go after more sales or profits.

5) The correct approach is to take actions that address the company's key issues embedded in the crisis points set out in the Growth Model. Increased sales and profits will be the result of these actions.

6) The set of crisis points and action steps relevant to a company's situation varies depending upon the particular growth phase the company is in.

7) Once the company's growth phase has been determined, crisis points and action steps may be fairly well defined.

After jotting these down, Jerry turned to the evaluation tool Mike had given him. For the next 15 minutes, Jerry worked feverishly. For each statement on the assessment tool, Jerry was required to assign a value according to the following:

2	Very true
1	Somewhat true
0	Not true at all

The results of his work follow:

OWNER/MANAGEMENT TEAM ASSESSMENT
Phase I—Entrepreneurial Start-Up

Numerical score
(2, 1 or 0):

2	Founders are running the company
0	Founders are technical achievers or market builders-usually not strong managers
2	Emphasis is on producing products or services and selling them
0	Minimal emphasis on management, systems, planning, etc.
1	Informal organization and communication structure
1	Long work hours-modest salaries
0	Management reacts mostly to customers rather than employees
0	Growth rate is greater than inflation, but moderate
0	Not clear who is in charge when there are two or more partners in the business
0	Conflicts between founders or partners
0	New employees not motivated by dedication
2	Poor accounting and cash control
2	Working capital shortages
0	Minimal financial planning
0	Little or no business planning
0	Temptation to diversify into unrelated businesses
10	**Total Phase I score**

Phase II—Entrepreneurial Expansion

*Numerical score
(2, 1 or 0):*

| 2 | Leader chosen and accepted |

| 0 | Often multiple locations, such as: sales, branch offices, warehouses |

| 2 | Detailed attention given to areas in addition to producing products or services and selling |

| 1 | Employee duties are more specialized, formally defined and communicated |

| 1 | Company becomes more impersonal |

| 1 | Growth rate faster than Phase I; sometimes accelerates to a very fast rate |

| 1 | Delegation is increasingly difficult for the leader |

| 0 | Access to the leader becomes difficult |

| 0 | Qualified managers are not permitted to make decisions in their technical areas |

| 1 | Managers are technically oriented and not accustomed to making their own decisions |

| 1 | Poor decisions are made in areas, such as: data processing, facilities expansion, hiring key employees, use of cash, financing |

| 0 | Problem solving is time consuming |

| 2 | Key employees become disenchanted and leave |

| 1 | Financial performance and control systems are often inadequate for sales volume |

| 1 | Shortages of management time and cash |

| 1 | Reactionary planning |

| 0 | Temptation to sustain faster growth so loyal employees will have opportunity |

| 0 | Temptation to diversify into unrelated businesses |

| 15 | **Total Phase II score** |

Phase III—Professional Management

Numerical score
(2, 1 or 0)

2	Necessary financial performance reporting and control systems in place and operational
1	Decentralized organization by function, product/service or location
1	Company has identity beyond the founder(s) and current leader
2	Short and intermediate term plans in place
2	Managers doing more managing than technical work
2	All elements critical to success bases are covered
2	Profit centers established
1	Growth rate moderate
0	Reaction to change becomes difficult-reaction time has increased
1	Senior management feels it is losing control-less contact with day-to-day operations
1	Increased vulnerability to outside factors, such as: government, unions, competition
1	Increased vulnerability to internal factors, such as: politics, outdated corporate culture, bureaucracy
0	Reaction to new business opportunities is cumbersome
2	Threatened by larger competitors
0	Little communication from the top
2	Need for longer range planning is evident, but resistance to doing it
1	Temptation to commence faster growth rate than company can absorb
21	**Total Phase III score**

Phase IV—Professional Management and Planning

Numerical score
(2, 1 or 0)

| 0 | Product groups/business units are treated as investment centers |

| 0 | Emphasis is on return on invested capital |

| 0 | Incentive compensation plans are in place |

| 0 | Generally cash is not a problem |

| 0 | Consistent financial performance is the norm |

| 1 | Planning is formalized and is a part of corporate culture |

| 2 | Company's culture is oriented to both sales and profits |

| 0 | Systems for information and control are in place |

| 1 | Some in-fighting exists among employees and management |

| 1 | Insufficient managerial training is a problem |

| 0 | Company's culture rewards those who do what they are told |

| 0 | Employees and lower management are suspicious of change |

| 0 | Low levels of internal motivation is a problem |

| 0 | Managers do not have authority equal to responsibility |

| 1 | Shortages of well trained people are a problem |

| 0 | Bureaucracy is a problem |

| 2 | Organization has vitality and momentum |

| 8 | **Total Phase IV score** |

When he was through scoring, the summary of his scores looked like this:

Ph I	Start up	10
Ph II	Entrepreneurial Expansion	15
Ph III	Professional Management	21
Ph IV	Professional Management and Planning	8

The above scores indicated that Cleveland Electronics was a **Phase III** company.

"*Aha,*" said Jerry to himself, "*a Phase III company. I just knew all of those management seminars I went to would pay off,*" his head told him in a congratulatory tone. "*So, based on what Mike's telling me, I've already been through the worst of the bad times. Maybe I pushed the panic button too early. I really think that Unisonictelcom's big five million dollar order is what's going to push us over the top. Good times are probably just around the corner.*"

With that, Jerry put his thoughts of business away and started reading the latest Carl Hiassen mystery novel he had picked up at a little bookstore down in Marathon. He couldn't wait to get back to the office and report the details of his trip to the management team.

"*Now,*" said Jerry to himself as he began to get into the book, "*down to some serious stuff. What's Skink going to fry up for dinner next?*"

Chapter 9

11:00 AM the next day. The entire management team of Cleveland Electronics was assembled at the large conference table in Jerry's office:

> Dave Kork, Controller
>
> Jason Pettibone, VP of sales
>
> Chuck Donaldson, VP of manufacturing, and
>
> Amy Langer, Jerry's administrative assistant.

Jerry had called all of them in at eight, and had been enthusiastically going over everything he and Mike Henderson had explored in Florida. As the group was about to break up, Jerry announced the conclusion he had come to on the way home on the plane:

"In short, folks, the worst is behind us. We've just come through our Phase II crisis points. We've spent the money, hired the right people, attended the seminars, and bought the right equipment. Good times are right around the corner."

Jerry looked triumphantly at his management team. But something was wrong. The managers weren't looking at him. At first, each manager just stared off into space. Then, after a few seconds, one or two looked at each other. Jerry, who couldn't stand the "dead air" or lack of eye contact finally asked: "What's the matter?"

"Weeeell, Jerry…" began Chuck Donaldson.

"Ah, you see…" said Jason Pettibone.

"Jerry, maybe we'd better meet after our meeting," said Dave Kork.

"Hey, folks, is something wrong?" asked Jerry, confused.

"Well, see, while you've been away, a couple of things have happened that we were going to talk about this morning—before we started talking about growth models and stuff. We thought that was why you called the meeting," said Chuck.

"What do you mean?" asked Jerry. "What kind of *stuff?*"

At that, everyone started talking at once:

"Two of the suppliers critical to the Unisonictelcom order say they won't be able to meet delivery dates for the next shipment deadline"—Chuck.

"Donny (the sales rep that helped Jerry sell the Unisonictelcom order) says he wants his standard commission on the deal instead of the one and a half percent we thought we agreed on"—Jason.

"We're almost maxed out on our bank line of credit and Rich (the banker) called twice wondering what we're doing with all the inventory we're showing on last quarter's balance sheet."—Dave.

"The assistant to Unisonictelcom's plant manager called late yesterday afternoon. They want to meet with you and Chuck. The reject rate on the last shipment was three and a quarter percent—more than double what they said we agreed to."—Amy.

"And to top it all off, the cost sheets on the Unisonictelcom order show we're losing money. About five point eight percent of every sales dollar we ship out of here"—Dave Kork and Chuck Donaldson, almost in unison.

Jerry and his managers spent the next 45 minutes discussing these issues—which were, of course, far more immediate "crises" than the ones Jerry and Mike were talking about down in the Keys. After discussing several temporary cures, the managers agreed to meet for breakfast the next morning to continue the attempts to resolve their immediate "crises."

The next morning, Chuck and Dave arrived a little early for breakfast. While waiting for the rest of the team to show up, they talked again about Henderson's Business Growth Model and how it might apply to Cleveland Electronics.

After a quick glance at the menu, Chuck said, "You know, I was thinking about all of the 'crises' we started to deal with yesterday. I think most if not all of them are related to the crisis points in Henderson's model."

"How so?" asked Dave.

"Take, for example, the two suppliers that can't deliver on time for us to make the next shipment on the Unisonictelcom order. I found out that one of the suppliers, Tabco, called two weeks ago and told Gail that they could deliver only 2,500 of the 3,100 connectors we'd need. Gail was going to tell parts and planning about it a couple of hours later when that person got in, but then she forgot. If we had a system where critical information like that was input and distributed to appropriate people in our production process, one of yesterday's fires wouldn't have happened."

"And," said Dave, "if Gail was operating with clear written instructions and if she had been properly trained in those instructions, we could have incorporated a policy where information like this was not only input into the computer, but, in planning's absence, should be communicated to someone like Paul Daniels—or another appropriate party."

"Right. Uh, oh, here comes Jerry."

"Morning, guys," greeted Jerry.

"Hi, boss."

Dave: "Say, Jerry, we were just talking about how yesterday's fires may be related to some of the things you and Mike were going over down in the Keys. I'm curious—did Mike help you fill out that questionnaire where you determined we were a Phase III company?"

"Why,…ah…ah…no. I filled it out on the plane on the way home," said Jerry.

"At the risk of losing my job," said Chuck, "do you think you may have been just a little bit biased when you filled it out?"

"Come on, Chuck, you've been a lot more critical of me than that…and you're still here," said Jerry with a smile. "I suppose that what you're suggesting is possible, but I don't think it could be off by much."

"What if all of us filled out the questionnaire, and compared our results to those you got?" offered Dave.

"Good idea," Chuck interjected.

Jerry thought a moment, and then expressed his opinion that this might be a good idea. As he was thinking, the rest of the management team arrived. Jerry outlined the discussion he, Dave and Chuck had just had, and the team agreed to complete their questionnaires and meet again in three days.

Jerry: "In the meantime, guys, how are we doing on yesterday's fires? Dave, what did Rich say when you called the bank?"

Chapter 10

Three days later. The management team meeting is in progress. A large white board has the following diagram:

		Jerry	Team
I	Start up	10	15
II	Entrep exp	15	24
III	Prof mgmt	21	6
IV	Prof mgt pln	8	4

The team was discussing the marked differences in scores, and what this meant to the company.

Most of the team members felt that Jerry's evaluation was biased, and Chuck, the plant manager and most vocal member of the team, was making a point:

"Look here, Jerry. You're saying that the statement that 'short and intermediate plans are in place' is **very true**. Where are these plans? I haven't seen one in over two years."

"Has it been that long?" Jerry asked. "The one I'm thinking about is the plan we did when the bank was thinking about giving us the new round of financing."

Dave and Amy both affirmed that the bank-financing package was the last time they had revised the annual operating plan.

"Jerry," said Chuck, "I think the questionnaire is looking for a current plan- one that we live by, monitor, revise as needed, and hold people accountable to. The one we did for the bank was just what you said-a piece of paper we had to prepare in order to get our line of credit increased."

"Chuck may be right," said Amy softly. "It seems like so much of what we do here is to please outsiders-bankers, suppliers, customers, OSHA, etc."

"OK, OK," said Jerry with a chuckle. "I'm willing to concede that you guys are probably more objective here than I. So, we've got a Phase II company facing a large order with a new customer that can make or break us. And I'm right back to where I was in the airport the day we made the big proposal to get the order. I'm afraid we're in 'way over our heads. What do we do?"

> "The plan we did for the bank was just what you said—a piece of paper we had to prepare in order to get our line of credit increased."

"First things first," said Dave. "It seems like we've handled all of the fires that broke out a couple of days ago on the Unisonictelcom order. That is, with the exception of the fact that we're going to lose about 6 % on the next shipment. It's too late to do anything about that."

"Are you sure?" Jerry.

"Yes." replied Dave. Then, very gently, Dave reminded Jerry "As you've told us Mike Henderson said to you, 'numbers are the end of the earnings process, not the beginning. Most often, they're the result of activities and actions, not the cause. It's the activities and actions a company does that generate the profit or loss.' And, in this case, Jerry, I'm afraid we're a little too late to avoid losing money on this shipment."

"Where do we go from here?" asked Jerry.

Jason said, "Didn't Henderson tell you where to go with this?"

> "...numbers are the end of the earnings process, not the beginning. Most often, they're the result of activities and actions, not the cause..."

"Not yet," replied Jerry. "I'll give him a call right after lunch."

Later that afternoon, Jerry put in a call to Henderson. Mike, who was in his office that day, was updated on the things that had happened at Cleveland Electronics since the meeting in the Keys. Jerry had just related the events of the morning meeting when Mike asked him,

"Jerry, what are your plans in terms of the next step in the process?"

"That's why I'm calling you, Mike."

Mike and Jerry then discussed the results of the management team's evaluation of Cleveland Electronics. They agreed the company was heavily in the throes of its Phase II crises. Although Jerry had tried his best in the last two years to build a management team and install systems, it seems as if his efforts never quite bore fruit. Mike explained that this wasn't at all unusual. Once a company "hits the wall," it is very hard to correct problems and return to profitability without help. And, of course, a focused, disciplined approach to implementing improvements.

"Jerry, do you still have copies of those slides we went over down in the Keys?"

"Well—uh—yeah. Yes. But I've got notes written all over them."

"Yes, and I seem to recall you had the name and telephone number of that waitress with the treasure coin written on those slides, also," chided Mike. "What was her name again?"

"Amber," said Jerry.

"Amber?" For half an instant, Mike's eyes took on a startled look. But then he snapped right back to business. Jerry, focused on the process of fixing his company and on the telephone besides, missed the look in Mike's eyes.

"Jerry, I'll e-mail you a clean copy of the presentation. When you get it, I want you to take the section on Phase II, starting with <u>Management Emphasis</u>, and distribute that section to your management team."

"Right," said Jerry. "Then what?"

"Then, you have a couple of meetings where you go through the slides."

"What these slides do, you see, is lay out the things your company will need to focus upon in order to clear its Phase II crisis points."

"I've got it so far. Then what?"

"Well, as you and the management team go through these slides, I would like you to circle the items which you agree are applicable as they relate to your company. When you have this done, phone me again."

"Sounds good, Mike," said Jerry. "I'll be in touch."

Chapter 11

A week later, Jerry and his team were following through on Henderson's recommendation. They were in a Holiday Inn a couple of miles from Cleveland Electronics. Jerry and Amy both thought the team needed to be away from all outside distractions for this next important step in the company's growth process.

After almost six hours, the team had marked up Henderson's slide show as follows:

Accounting & Finance:

—Improvement and expansion of basic accounting and financial reporting systems

- Financial statements
- Cash flow projections
- Operating budget
- Capital budget

Accounting & Finance *(continued)*:

—Departmental budgeting

—Return on investment accounting (ROI)

—Create controllership position

—Solidify controllership position

—Financial data interpretation

Systems and IT:

- Needs determination
- Hardware/Software selection

- Management/Technical personnel selection
- Core systems

Sales and Marketing:
- Product life-cycle planning
- Create marketing function
- Analysis of competition
- One-year sales & marketing plan

Operations:
- Facilities and equipment planning
- Product (operations) control
- Finished goods inventory control
- Cost accounting
- One-year production plan
- Produce or out-source

Human resources:
- Build an aligned management team
- Turn technicians into managers
- Plan and implement managerial accountability
- Determine responsibilities and expectations of key roles
- Recruit key personnel
- Broaden external business awareness

Personnel:
- Incentive sales compensation
- Management and technical training
- Employee performance evaluation process
- Compliance with government requirements
- One-year manpower plan

Business strategy and planning:

- One to three-year business plan
- Strategy emphasis

    —*Growth, Survival and Profitability*

- Product or services strategy
- Design action plans as part of business planning
- Goal: Become a Phase III Company[2]

The team then made a list from the above slides. The items that everyone agreed needed to be worked on were:

*Accounting and finance

—Operating budget

—Capital budget

—Financial data interpretation

*Systems and IT

—Management/technical personnel selection

—Core systems

*Sales and marketing

—One-year sales plan

*Operations

—Operations control

—Finished goods inventory control

*Management and leadership

—Build an aligned management team

—Determine responsibilities and expectations of key jobs

*Personnel

—Incentive sales compensation

—Management and technical training

---

2 Adapted from a presentation, *Evolution of a Business,* by Gleeson, Sklar, Sawyers & Cumpata, LLP, 1997.

*Business strategy and planning

    —One to three-year business plan

    —Product or services strategy

    —Design action plans as part of business planning

"Wow!" said Amy. "Those are a lot of items."

"About 15, it looks like," said Dave.

"No wonder they made you an accountant," kidded Jason.

Chuck then said, "Well, how do we figure out which ones to work on first?"

Jerry said, "You know, I don't think Henderson covered that. But doesn't it make sense that we should try and prioritize the points and work on the most important ones first?"

"Sounds like a plan, Jerry," murmured Chuck, Jason, Amy and the others. So for the next hour, they discussed the points and tried to come up with a ranking. Finally, Chuck spoke up:

"It's almost four thirty, and we've just wasted the last hour. Are you sure Henderson didn't tell you how to prioritize these?"

"No," said Jerry. "Tell you what. Let's break out the beer and cocktails and relax a few minutes. Amy, you give Mike a call and try to get him on the speaker phone in here."

"Right, chief," replied Amy. "And could you fix me a Bailey's on the rocks, please?"

Chapter 12

Ten minutes later, the team was sitting around the conference room table. Mike Henderson was on the speakerphone, and they had just exchanged pleasantries and got the usual bantering over with when Jerry offered,

"Hey, Mike, my team is all sitting around here with drinks in hand. Why don't you fix yourself a cocktail before we get started?"

"I'd be happy to, Jerry, especially since we started on your dime a couple of minutes ago," said Mike. "But it won't take that long to pour another cup of coffee."

"We'll wait," offered Dave.

When Mike got back to the phone, he opened with, "How far did you get on identifying the items you'll need to resolve your crisis points?"

Chuck replied, "We listed them all out. Dave counted 15 items. We assumed the thing to do next was to discuss and prioritize them and then start working from the top of the list."

Mike said, "Sounds like a very logical plan. I'll bet Jerry didn't come up with it."

"No, we all did," laughed Chuck. "But we've just wasted an hour trying to do our list. We got nowhere."

Mike replied, "That's because you didn't go about it the right way."

"What do you mean?" asked Jerry. "You said the way we wanted to go about it sounded **logical**."

"Jerry, don't whine," said Mike. "Here's what we used to call in the Army a 'teaching point.' Just because something sounds logical doesn't mean its right. It wasn't that way in school, and it surely isn't that way in business."

> "Just because something sounds logical doesn't mean its right."

"Mike, I hope I know the answer to the next question. Do **you** know where we should go from here?" asked Jerry.

"Yes," replied Mike. "But it's getting late, and I don't know if we really have time to get into it right now."

"Just give us the two minute version," said Jerry impatiently.

Mike replied, "Well, the whole process has to start with your business plan, since that plan is the key document in achieving alignment in your company. Therefore, the business plan comes first. Once you have made progress on it, the other items can be worked on as well. However, it's important to point out that, when it comes to fixing your company, remember, its not just one thing. You will need to have several of these Growth Model items com-

> "...it's important to point out that, when it comes to fixing your company, remember, it's not just one thing."

pleted and implemented before seeing a significant bottom-line impact."

"So we start with the business plan?" asked Amy.

"Right. And to do that—Jerry, flip to the last couple of slides I gave you down in Marathon. That will get you and the team started."

"Will do, Mike. And thank you very, very much," said Chuck.

"You are most welcome," replied Mike. "If you get stuck, telephone me and I will try to help."

With that, the conference call was terminated, the team agreed to set a time for the next meeting, cocktails were finished, and the office lights went out after a very long, exhausting day for all.

Chapter 13

Early the next morning, Jerry reviewed the slides on Business Planning that Mike referred to the night before. **The reader will find these at the end of the book as Exhibit D.** As he was going over the slides, he had a couple of questions, and so Jerry called Henderson.

"Hello," answered Mike.

"Mike, its Jerry. I had a couple of questions on these *Ten Point Planning Process* slides you gave me."

"Well, Jerry, you're going to have to hurry up. I'm just leaving to go out of town. My auto parts distribution client needs help again."

"Is that the one you did the turn around on a couple of years ago?" asked Jerry.

"Yes."

"Mike, if you don't mind my asking, why do they still need help?" inquired Jerry.

"Well, you see, they got through their Phase III crisis and grew from $25 million to over $60 million in sales. However, a few months ago they bought out a smaller distributor on the East Coast. They need help in getting the new acquisition assimilated into their corporate structure and ways of doing business. Now, Jerry, how can I help you?"

"Mike, I'm having a problem with the first couple of steps of your planning process-the steps having to do with mission, vision, core values, and guiding principles. This stuff sounds like its right out of a textbook. I'm having a hard time seeing how this kind of 'ivory tower' stuff is going to pull Cleveland Electronics out of the problems we've been having," said Jerry.

"Jerry, I'm really pressed for time here. But, what did I tell you were the two keys to every company's success?"

"Uh...uh..." Jerry's brain went into high gear, struggling to remember what Mike had told him down in the Keys. All of a sudden, he remembered—"planning and execution?" Jerry advanced, tentatively.

> "...The two keys to every company's success—PLANNING and EXECUTION..."

"That's exactly right," said Mike. "And those first steps in the planning process are your initial steps in developing focus. Jerry, I really can't spend any more time right now. Tell you what...I helped your buddy Bruce through this stuff once, and Bruce and I just went through it again a couple of months ago. Why don't you call him and have him coach you through the process?"

"Sounds good, Mike," said Jerry enthusiastically.

"And while you're at it Jerry, ask Bruce again if this stuff worked for him," said Mike.

Jerry's next call was to Bruce. He was lucky. Bruce was in his office working. They caught up on each other's lives since the last time both of them talked. Jerry related the conversation he'd just had with Henderson.

"Anyway, Bruce, what can you tell me about this business planning stuff?" Jerry asked.

Bruce replied,

"A major benefit of business planning is that, if done correctly, the finished plan is an important step in creating **alignment** among the five key elements of your company:

-Organization

-Operations

-Employees

-Sales and marketing

-Finance and management

When these are all working together, and are in phase with one another, the company makes money. Understand so far?"

"What do you mean by 'in phase'?" asked Jerry.

"I'll leave it to Henderson to go through it with you in detail some other time, Jer. I don't want us to get distracted. But, quickly, did Henderson go through his growth model with you?"

"Yes."

"Remember the four growth phases Companies go through?"

"Yes."

"OK. When you break your company down into its five key elements, Henderson can tell you what phase of growth each element is at. When all five key elements are in the same phase, the company's said to be 'in phase.' But, let's get back to your question on doing a business plan," coached Bruce.

"Yeah, right" said Jerry. "It says here to develop a mission statement, vision statement, core values and guiding principles. And, I have to tell you: I know lots of companies who came up with mission statements and vision statements over the years. Including Cleveland Electronics. And when I get together with other business owners and we discuss mission statements and vision statements, we just laugh. It seems like none of us can figure out how these statements have done any good except to make the consultants who probably thought this stuff up in the first place rich!"

"That's exactly what I told Henderson the first time he went through business planning with me," said Bruce.

"And what did Mr. Smart Mouth Billy Bass say to that?" smirked Jerry.

"He said the reason mission statements and vision statements never did much good for most small companies is because that was all the long range planning most of these companies ever did. He said that in order for these things to do any good at all, companies have to go ahead and complete the other nine-and-one-half steps of the Business Planning

> "…the reason mission statements and vision statements never did much good for most small companies is because that was all the long range planning most of these companies ever did."

Process. And then you have to implement these plans. In fact, he had a funny little phrase he used...let's see...oh, yeah...

'In order for your

Vision statement and Mission statement

to show up on your

financial statement,

a company needs to complete and implement the other nine and one-half steps of the planning process.'"

"Well, actually, the whole thing's starting to make sense to me," said Jerry. "In order for everyone in the company to be aligned, it helps to know what the company at its core is all about. And if this is written down, it's easier to communicate to all of the employees."

"Not just the employees," said Bruce, "but to customers, vendors, bankers, your attorney, accountant, and other outside advisors as well."

"Yep. Makes perfect sense to me now," said Jerry.

"Scary," said Bruce. "All right, I've got to go make some dough for my company now."

"Thanks for the info, pal," said Jerry. "If I have any questions, I'll catch up to you later."

Chapter 14

Later that day, Jerry met with his management team. Since they had worked on company mission statements in the past, the work at first went rather quickly. The team basically went over the mission and vision statements that had been developed five to ten years ago. A couple of team members expressed the same misgivings Jerry had about the value of these statements. Jerry related the discussion he and Bruce had. That seemed to satisfy the managers temporarily, and the meeting moved on.

Amy then said, "Now, on to the hard part. Core values and guiding principles. We've never had these before. Where do we start?"

Chuck Donaldson chimed in. "Remember that plant managers seminar I went to a couple of years ago? We spent about a day with one of those 'corporate development' consultants. He spent a lot of time talking about core values and guiding principles."

Dave asked, "Do you remember anything about what he said?"

Chuck replied, "Yes, quite a bit. The consultant's talk was very interesting, because I had never heard anything like this before and, quite frankly, I thought that some of the problems we were having at the time could have been solved by what the consultant recommended."

"What did he recommend?" asked Jerry.

"He said every company should write down their core values and guiding principles, and publish them. You know, make sure employees, customers and vendors are aware of what these values and principles are," said Chuck.

"Sounds a lot like what Bruce told me this morning," said Jerry.

"The other thing I remember," said Chuck, "is that you don't just sit around in a room and make up these things."

"Then how do we get them?" asked Jason, VP of Sales, who had been pretty quiet throughout the meeting.

Chuck replied, "Well, as I recall, the consultant said that all companies have values and principles. In small companies like Cleveland Electronics, the company gets these mainly from the owner/founder."

"Then our job is simply to identify these values and principles and write them down?" asked Dave.

"Right," said Chuck.

Jerry and the team discussed the foregoing conversation for ten or fifteen minutes. Finally, since the morning was growing old, and the team needed to get back to running the business, they agreed to adjourn for a few days.

"In the meantime," said Chuck, "I'll look through my files. I think that consultant gave us several examples of core values and guiding principles from other companies."

"Yeah," said Jerry. "And I'll get the ones from Bruce's company. We can copy and distribute all of this to each of you in the next day or so."

"Great," said Amy. "And I'll set up the next meeting for…?"

"Five or six days from now. Make it for two hours," said Jerry.

With that, the session adjourned.

Chapter 15

The next day, Jerry thought again about the manager's meeting. He looked at the Business Planning slides again, and noted that Item 2 called for defining the business you are in.

"Easy," declared Jerry. "We make electronic components."

"Maybe that was too easy," Jerry's mind suggested. *"I wonder if that's the definition Mike is looking for. I don't want to look stupid at the next management team meeting. Maybe I'd better call Mike and ask him if my definition's OK."*

Jerry then called Mike. Henderson's office, home and cell phones all indicated that he was out of the office but would be checking messages.

"Damn!" Jerry said softly. "I guess its time to try Bruce again."

Jerry buzzed Amy and asked her to set up a lunch with Bruce. Amy reported back in a few minutes with the good news—Bruce and Jerry would be having lunch.

"Eagle Inn. Eleven forty-five," said Amy.

"Great!" exclaimed Jerry.

   *   *   *

The entrees had just been finished and coffee was ordered. Up to this point, lunch had consisted of catching up on families, social life, and sports teams. Finally, Jerry got around to business.

"Say, Bruce, did you bring your company's core values and guiding principles?"

"Sure did. Here they are. Why don't you read them over and tell me what you think?" asked Bruce.

Jerry read over the two pieces of paper that Bruce had given him. On the first page were four words:

Precision   **Honesty**   **Reliability**   **Value**

Page two had these eight sentences:

- We will be absolutely honest in dealings with our employees and customers

- All product delivered to customers will exceed tolerances specified by the customer

- Any defects noted by a customer will if at all possible be corrected within 48 hours

- Our price will not always be the cheapest, but it will always represent the best value

- Ownership will discuss decisions with affected managers and employees wherever possible, but all decisions related to personnel will be made by ownership.

- We will treat our employees and customers with the respect and honor they deserve.

- In the event of a conflict between customer and employee needs, every attempt will be made to accommodate our employee's commitments and convenience.

- However, if such conflicts cannot be resolved, the customer's needs shall come first.

"Well?" asked Bruce after a few minutes.

"Gees, Bruce," said Jerry; "the first thing that strikes me is that these two pieces of paper sound just like **you**. Are you sure these are your **company's** core values and guiding principles?"

"They're the company's, all right," said Bruce. "But remember who founded, grew and shaped my company."

"Oh. Right," replied Jerry. "My production guy, Chuck, said something about the company's values and principles following the owner's. On to the next question, Bruce. What does Henderson mean in the Business Planning slides when he says 'Define the business you are in'?"

"That's a tricky one," said Bruce. "When I first tried to do this, I came up with a short definition of what the company did—plastic injection mold maker. But, when I defined my business that way, I didn't find anything useful about the definition. So Henderson and I got together, because I was stuck."

"That's good," said Jerry.

"Huh? Why's that good?" puzzled Bruce.

"Cause I'm stuck, too, and everyone knows I'm smarter than you," jibed Jerry.

"Not just smarter, but handsomer, too," countered Bruce. "And if you're so smart, how come you asked me to help you out on this?"

"Touché, buddy" replied Jerry.

"Right. So, anyway," continued Bruce, "Henderson said I should look at what I did through the eyes of the customer. What part does my company play in the customer's business? Where does my company start adding value to the customer's business—and where does it end?"

> "What part does my company play in the customer's business? Where does my company start adding value to the customer's business—and where does it end?"

"Wow," exclaimed Jerry. "That's going to require some thought."

"No kidding," said Bruce. "When Henderson and I first covered this, I didn't have a management team. So, he and I kicked my business definition around for a couple of weeks before we finally came up with what we both agreed was a good, working definition."

"So," said Jerry. "You went from plastic injection mold maker to...?"

"A service business that helps its customers in the development, design and fabrication of tooling for thermoset plastic applications," replied Bruce.

"Nice," responded Jerry. "I guess I should bring the managers in on this one."

"That'd be a good idea," said Bruce. "Now, Jerry, would you hurry up and pay the tab? I've got a one thirty tee-off time."

Chapter 16

Jerry and Chuck, his plant manager, were having lunch a few days later. They had been going over some manufacturing issues and discussing the Unisonictelcom order. Chuck and Jerry had just ordered coffee when Chuck suddenly changed the subject.

"Have you noticed a change in the way Jason (Jerry's VP of Sales) has been acting lately?" asked Chuck.

Jerry replied, "No, not really…wait. Wait a minute. I **have** noticed that I've had less contact with him in the past few weeks. Almost like he's been avoiding me. And, Amy's mentioned that when she's walked into his office a couple of times recently, he's apparently been on telephone calls he didn't want her to hear."

"Huh," said Chuck.

"Why did you bring it up?" asked Jerry.

"Well," said Chuck, "I've noticed him talking to a couple of engineering types out in the plant. More than once or twice. When I first noticed it, I remembered that the whole time I've been here, I had only seen him actually in the plant a handful of times."

"That's interesting." said Jerry. "And I just realized something else. Jason's been awfully quiet during our team meetings."

"That's for sure," replied Chuck. "Which is really unlike Jason. He's usually more than happy to bend your ear for 30 minutes or an hour on just about any subject he's got an opinion on."

"Maybe I'd better talk to him," replied Jerry.

"I think that would be a good idea," said Chuck.

The two finished their discussion and coffee and headed for the office.

*   *   *

Three o'clock that afternoon…

Jerry and Amy had just finished going over Jerry's schedule for the next few days when Jason knocked on Jerry's office door.

"Jer?" asked Jason.

"Oh, hi, Jason, Come on in. How are things?" asked Jerry in the most welcoming tone he could muster.

"Oh. OK. Say, how about you and I going out for a drink?" asked Jason tentatively.

"Well, any other time, Jason, I'd love to," said Jerry. "But I promised the family I'd be home by five o'clock tonight."

"OK," sighed Jason. "I guess now's as good a time as any. Jerry, I'm leaving the company."

"What?" asked Jerry in a shocked tone. "Jason, come on over here and let's sit down."

The two moved to a corner of Jerry's office with a couple of soft chairs, coffee table and overstuffed couch. As they settled into the arrangement, Jerry in a chair, Jason on the couch, Jerry noticed a warm feeling in his face and a tingling in his ears.

"All right, Jason, what's up?"

"Well, Jerry, to make a long story short, I just can't work here any more. You, the management team and I have been talking about all of our problems for weeks, and nothings getting done. My customers are complaining louder and more frequently than ever about orders not shipping, details are getting dropped, people are promising to get back to them and then nothing happens, etc., etc., etc., etc."

"Jason, you never told me you were unhappy here," replied Jerry.

"Jerry, your whole focus these past five weeks has been the Unisonictelcom order and the 'fires' myself, you and the rest of the management team have spent time putting out. And on top of that, we're running around trying to respond to a bunch of stuff some management consultant says that we have to do in order to make the company better. With all of these distractions, you wouldn't have listened even if I tried to communicate how unhappy and frustrated I've become. So, consider **right now** to be the beginning of my two week notice period—unless you want me to leave before then."

"Damn," said Jerry. "I don't know. Let's discuss this some more."

Jerry and Jason spent the next hour elaborating on Jason's unhappiness, whether Jerry could do anything to get Jason to change his mind, and transition plans. At the end of the meeting, they decided to stay with the two weeks notice, but if Jason felt he had provided an adequate transition before then, he could leave before his two weeks were up. As they were having these discussions, Jerry kept thinking about the confidentiality, employment, and non-competition agreements he and his lawyer were talking about having the sales reps and managers sign. *"Oh, well,"* thought Jerry, *"too late now."*

The meeting ended with the two shaking hands uncomfortably and Jason leaving Jerry's office.

As soon as Jason was gone, Amy came in. "Well, what'd he want?"

Jerry replied. "He just quit."

Amy replied, "We were getting hints…"

Jerry said, "Yes, I know. But I never realized how unhappy he had become. I wonder how the rest of our employees feel?"

Amy replied, "Jerry, we've talked about this. Many of the other employees have some of the same feelings as Jason. But they don't leave. Probably because they're either more loyal or less marketable than Jason."

"I suppose you're right," said Jerry. "I'm going home to cry in my beer. Notify the other team members that he's leaving with two week's notice, and that we need to do everything we can to assure a smooth transition. For right now, I'll take over the VP-sales job. Also, draft up a general announcement to all employees that I can look at in the morning."

"Right," said Amy. "Anything else?"

"Not right now. See you in the morning."

Chapter 17

9:00 PM that same day. Jerry and his wife Gina are lying in bed reading after a long and tiring day for both of them.

At dinner that night, it became apparent that the only bright spot in the family's day occurred when Jerry and Gina's daughter Jacqueline received her latest essay back from her teacher with an "A."

"And you both know how few 'A's' Miss Sylvester gives out," said Jacqueline proudly.

"That's wonderful, honey," exclaimed the proud father. "And what was your essay about?"

Jacqueline and Gina both giggled then broke into uncontrollable young girl laughter.

"Huh," said Jerry. "It must have been a really funny essay, if both of you are laughing this hard."

"Oh, it was," said Gina. "Tell him, Jacqueline."

"Dad, do you remember April Fools Day?" asked Jacqueline sweetly.

"Oh, you didn't. Don't **even** tell me you wrote about that in your essay," threatened Jerry.

"Yep. The title of my essay was "April Fool and Nobody's Home." Miss Sylvester said it was the funniest 500 word story she's read in three years," said Jacqueline proudly.

Back in the bedroom, Jerry and Gina had a last laugh over Jacqueline's essay, and then talked about Jason's leaving the company.

"Jerry," asked Gina, "do you think all these things you're doing with Henderson and Bruce are going to fix the company?"

"I don't know," said Jerry. "All I really know right now is that, if they are fixing the company, I wish things would start to **visibly** improve. And fast."

"Well, I seem to remember your saying that Henderson said things might take a few months to improve—even after major improvements to your company's management infrastructure had been made," remarked Gina.

"Yeah, but…" remarked Jerry.

"Do you think you should try and speed up the process?" asked Gina. "You know, spend more time working on the Growth Model with the management team?"

"That's easy to say, tough to do," replied Jerry. "Don't forget, each of us still has to do our jobs running the company every day."

"I have an idea. Why don't you get the whole team out of the office for two or three days—you know, have, like, a…"

"…like a retreat," finished Jerry. "Yeah. Not a bad idea. Glad I thought of it," Jerry kidded.

"Here we go again, 'Mr. Takes All the Credit'," pouted Gina.

"In fact," mused Jerry, "if I can get hold of Henderson tomorrow, maybe we can all go down to his place in the Keys. That way, he'll be available to answer our questions, slide us through any rough spots, and facilitate the whole meeting."

"Right," said Gina. "If Mike would do that, it would really speed things up."

"Well, I'll just have to get hold of him tomorrow," said Jerry. "Thanks for the great idea, Sweetie."

"You're welcome."

With that, Jerry and Gina rolled over and prepared for sleep. As Jerry drifted away into slumber, *he began dreaming of the silver Cobb coin…*

Chapter 18

As soon as Jerry got to his office the next day, he started the balls in motion. The management team (less Jason) was called together, rallied to the cause, and became revved up at Jerry's idea of putting the Mike Henderson project in high gear.

Jerry had Gina track down Henderson.

Jerry proceeded to catch Mike up on the events of the last few days, and the progress he and the management team had been making using Bruce as a fill in for Mike.

"But now, Mike," implored Jerry, "we really need the big gun back. We thought we'd like to have a management team retreat, and have you run it. That way, we can finish our growth model tasks quickly, and get the company back on track as quickly as possible."

"That sounds like a good idea, Jerry." replied Mike. "Let me check my schedule and other commitments. I can call you back. Where will you be around one o'clock your time tomorrow?"

"I can be anywhere you want me to be," replied Jerry.

"OK, then be by your office phone around one. I'll give you a call then and let you know my decision," said Mike.

"Take care," Mike.

*   *   *

The next day, 1:00 PM, Jerry's office.

The phone rang right on schedule. Mike & Jerry spent several minutes making plans for the management team's trip down to Marathon. Since Mike's place was small, the team would stay at a nearby Holiday Inn. The daily sessions would take place at Mike's house or at a small meeting room in the hotel. After setting a date two weeks in the future, Mike remarked, "Jerry, I had a couple of thoughts that could help us get this show on the road a little more quickly."

"I'm all ears," replied Jerry.

"Perhaps I should give you folks some homework to get done before we meet down in the Keys. That way, the whole process will move more efficiently once we get down there."

"Great," said Jerry. "What's our assignment?"

"Take a look at your <u>Ten Point Planning Process</u> slide:

Ten Point Planning Process

1) Determine mission/vision/core values/guiding principles

2) Define the business you are in

3) **Set growth goals: Phase I, Phase II, Phase III**

4) **Determine key jobs and get the right people in them. Define the management team.**

5) **Determine what is needed to get harmony in the management team and/or family**

6) **Define manager accountability**

7) **Set financial goals to get a balance among:**

   -Profit

   -Cash flow

   -Equity

8) Identify core systems and determine what is needed to make them work

9) Identify industry trends and set product goals (stars and cash cows)

10) Create action plans: Assign responsibilities, budgets and target dates

"You've already done Step 1, the part about mission/vision/core values/guiding principles. I understand from Bruce that the two of you have had some discussions about the second step; defining the business you are in. Is that right?" asked Mike.

"We've talked, but I really haven't finished this step," replied Jerry.

"All right," said Mike. "So the first homework assignment is to share what you and Bruce have discussed with the management team, and have each team member think about what business the company's in. Then, when we all get down to the Keys, we can talk about it some more and document your decision. Can you remember that?"

"I'm taking notes," Jerry replied.

"All right," said Mike. "Now, take a look at steps 3 through 7 of the *Ten Point Planning Process*. Homework assignment number two is for all of you to think about issues raised by these steps. You can even discuss these among yourselves before we all get together. Got it?"

"Right," said Jerry. "Although, I'm not sure how comfortable or candid we're going to be discussing the key jobs of the team, who's a fit, who's not, and what to do about it."

"That's perfectly OK," said Mike. "The important thing is to get everyone's thoughts focused so our discussion down in Marathon will be as productive as possible."

Jerry replied, "OK, I've written down that homework assignment. What's the next one?"

"The next and last one is to start working on what might be the most important step of all. Good old 'Number Eight'."

Jerry referred again to his *Ten Point Planning Process* slide. "You mean, 'Identify core systems and determine what is needed to make them work'?"

"Yes" said Mike. "Infrastructure."

"Infrastructure?" asked Jerry.

"Infrastructure," said Mike again.

"Mike, you might be a little confused by that treatment program you're going through," said Jerry. I'm not a road builder—I'm the guy who owns the electronic component manufacturer, remember?"

"Very funny, Jerry. But infrastructure means more than just roads and streets in a town or subdivision. To cut to the chase, infrastructure is a key component in solving all of those crises you've been having lately," Mike said.

> "...infrastructure is a key component in solving all of those crises you've been having lately..."

"Really?" asked Jerry. "How?"

"Let me use an example," said Mike.

"A couple of months ago, I was working with the owners of a company that was having severe cash flow problems. I recommended that they do a complete financial forecast, including the most important element, the cash flow forecast. A forecast like this, if completed and updated on a regular basis, is part of a company's infrastructure."

"Well," continued Mike, "the owners went on and on about how the most important element of the forecast, sales, was impossible to predict. We spent 20 minutes or so on how, although they might be able to see a week or two into the future, anything beyond that was pure guesswork. I offered to teach them techniques and systems to get beyond this, but they weren't ready to listen."

"This is starting to sound like my company," remarked Jerry suspiciously.

"Well it wasn't," assured Mike. "This was a printing company. Anyway, at the meeting one of the owners jumped in with…

'Look, Mike, what we're really looking for is help in cutting our expenses. Can you do anything to help us out there?'

"I then asked the owners what their largest controllable cost was. 'Labor,' they replied. Well, I said, when it comes to labor in this situation, you have two ways to go. One way is to reduce the number of employees on each shift. The other way is to eliminate one or more shifts entirely."

"You should have heard those owners squawk! 'Eliminate a shift? We can't possibly do that! Think of the message it would send to our sales reps and customers! Besides, what do we do if we eliminate a shift and then we get busy again? We need to always be ready to serve the needs of our customers, or pretty soon there won't be any customers left to worry about!'"

"Gentlemen, you're absolutely right, I said, trying to calm the discussion down. You wouldn't want to eliminate a shift if sales were going to go back up in the next two or three months. Yet, if you could eliminate the third shift, you'd save far more dollars than if you only reduced the number of employees on each shift, because along with getting rid of the shift, you get rid of supervision and other costs attributable to shift overhead. *Now do you see the value of a good sales forecast?*"

"Oh," said Jerry. "You know, Mike, we've had the same discussion many times around my company. And we don't forecast either—for the same reasons the printer gave you."

Mike replied, "Jerry, I've got news for you. Making money in manufacturing, and maybe in a lot of other industries as well, is all about matching <u>capacity</u> with <u>demand</u>. And you can't do that without knowing both of these key elements. In fact, a great deal of a manufacturer's infrastructure needs to be concerned with these two elements."

> "Making money in manufacturing, and maybe in a lot of other industries as well, is all about matching <u>capacity</u> with <u>demand</u>."

"I'm starting to get the picture," said Jerry. "Can you give me other examples of infrastructure?"

"Before we leave the above example," said Mike, "note that it could be that the core systems Step Eight is talking about are the systems at your company that relate to <u>capacity</u> and <u>demand</u>."

"Anyway," Mike continued, "it seems like I'm going to have to give you more meat to work with, Jerry."

"I think that'd be a good idea," replied Jerry.

"Why don't you go have a quick cup of coffee," said Mike. "In the meantime, I'll fax you a list of examples of company infrastructure."

When Jerry went to the fax after his coffee break, he found this list:

Examples of Infrastructure

Employees

—Personnel manual

—Standard personnel action forms

—Employment history form

—Job descriptions

—Written performance evaluations

—Formal employee counseling/goal setting process

Operations

—Machinery utilization reports

—Job scheduling system

—Work center production reports

—Job costing system

—Follow up system on actual v. estimated costs

—Delivery due date tracking system

—Material/Enterprise requirements planning system

—Daily stock status reports

Organization

—Organization chart

—Written business plan with accountabilities

—Strategic planning base

—Documented succession plans

—Emergency/disaster plans

Sales/marketing

—Sales projection/plan

—Effectiveness measures for ad campaigns, programs

—Competitive analysis

—Jobs bid/jobs won/jobs lost tracking system

Finance and management

—Monthly financial statements

—Weekly or daily "flash reports"

—Annual/monthly budgets, updated

—Monthly management's discussion of operating results

—Five-year financial projections

—Five-year capital budget

—Actual v. benchmarks for key indicators

"So, Mike, how do these relate to what we were talking about—capacity and demand?"

"For example, Jerry, these are the types of systems that would relate to your core issues of **capacity** and **demand**:

* Machinery utilization reports

* Order scheduling

* Detailed sales forecasts

* System of accountability for actual versus forecast sales."

"All right, Mike, I get the picture. But is there any way to prioritize which systems we're going to work on first?"

"In fact, Jerry, there is," replied Mike. "And you're going to love this next piece of wisdom."

"And why is that?" asked Jerry.

"Because, Jerry, we're actually going to talk about the problems you observed and which drove you to ask for my help in the first place," said Mike.

"You mean instead of all this consulting talk about core systems, growth models, mission statements, infrastructure, and all the rest?" asked Jerry.

"Yes," said Mike. "Because you see, Jerry, things like fouling up orders, running out of cash, creating bank overdrafts, losing money on significant orders, mishandling customer inquiries, etc. aren't the problems, they're the symptoms. The 'consulting talk' as you call it, is aiming at fixing the problems-the causes-of the symptoms you've been noticing."

> "…things like fouling up orders, running out of cash, creating bank overdrafts, losing money on significant orders, mishandling customer inquiries, etc. aren't the PROBLEMS, they're the SYMPTOMS."

"All right, all right," said Jerry impatiently. "But how does this all fit together?"

Mike continued:

"For purposes of homework assignment number three, have your people list all of the problems, or symptoms, the company's been having. Then, discuss these problems and decide among yourselves what types of **core systems** would have prevented these symptoms from occurring. A lot of what you'll find yourselves doing is actually discussing changes or improvements to your existing systems, since, as you are probably aware, all companies have some infrastructure. It's just that when 'symptoms' start occurring regularly, it's a signal that existing infrastructure is inadequate. It may simply need to be refined, or added on to, or replaced in order for the symptoms to go away."

> "...when 'symptoms' start occurring regularly, it's a signal that existing infrastructure is inadequate. It may simply need to be refined, or added on to, or replaced in order for the symptoms to go away."

"Sounds like a plan, Mike," said Jerry. "Is there anything else we should be doing?"

Mike replied, "I think three homework assignments in the next two weeks are more than enough. After all, you still have to keep the company in business, right?"

"You bet," said Jerry.

"OK, then. See you in the Keys."

Chapter 19

Over the next two weeks, Jerry and his team followed up on Mike's homework assignments. The day before taking off for the Keys, Jerry and the managers were having a final meeting, going over their homework assignments and making final arrangements for the big event.

They were finishing up their discussion and were almost ready to get back to the day-to-day business of running the company. Before they broke up, Jerry asked Amy, "What's the weather forecast for the Keys?"

Amy replied, "I checked the internet this morning. Sunny and humid, highs between 80 and 85 every day."

"Uh, oh," said Jerry.

"What do you mean by that," asked Dave, who was surprised at Jerry's reaction.

Jerry answered, "It sounds like perfect fishing weather."

"Uh, oh," the team exclaimed in unison, since by now they had all learned of Mike's passion for fishing.

"We'll just have to keep a close watch on Mr. Mike," a few of the team members exclaimed as they were leaving Jerry's office.

Chapter 20

After dinner that evening, Jerry went up to his room to pack. As he folded a pair of shorts to put in his bag, an old, washed-out piece of paper fell out of the pocket. It was one of Mike's slides. And when Jerry turned it over, a penned name and phone number was still barely legible:

Amber   (305) 555-2649

Jerry's thoughts went back to the night he met Amber in the restaurant. He thought about how excited Gina was going to be when she saw her birthday present. A genuine 1733 piece-of-eight! Off of a real Spanish treasure ship!

"Gee," thought Jerry, *"I wonder if Amber knows the name of the ship the coin came from? I'll have to remember to ask her...."*

"Honey—what are you thinking about?" Gina's words abruptly broke in on Jerry's flashback.

"Oh...uh...just thinking about the trip tomorrow," stammered Jerry.

"Are you sure that's <u>all</u> you were thinking about?" asked Gina, noticing Jerry's blush and his apparent high state of distraction.

Jerry saw her looking. "Well, to tell you the truth, dear, I was also thinking about that night at the airport hotel when you..."

Gina drew closer, and kissed her husband passionately.

Jerry's packing had to wait until early the next morning before the cab picked him up for his flight.

Chapter 21

3:00 PM the next day. The weather back in Cleveland was horrible—twelve degrees and snowing. It was a whole different picture where Jerry, Mike and the crew were gathered, however. The thermometer attached to the side of the Tiki bar in the Marathon Holiday Inn said 82 degrees, the sun was shining, and a ten mph breeze out of the south was softly blowing Amy's long brown hair.

"Folks, its good to have you down," said Mike as he finished a swallow of his Diet Pepsi.

"It's great to be here," said Dave Kork. "But then again, anywhere is better than sitting behind a stack of general ledger printouts in my office and watching the snow pile up on the window sill."

"You bet," echoed Jerry and Chuck.

"Mike, what exactly are we going to be doing for the three days we're down here?" asked Jerry.

"If I told you everything now, Jerry, we wouldn't have half the fun we'd have otherwise," said Mike. "But, I will tell you what we want to accomplish. How's that?"

"Fair enough," replied Jerry.

"OK. The main thing we're going to accomplish is to lay out framework and action steps to improve your company's planning and execution. We're going to do that by finishing the steps suggested by the Business Growth Model, and by providing some additional training so that you folks can finish fixing the company when we return to Cleveland."

"Wait a minute, Mike. You've said all along that **you** were going to fix the company," replied Jerry.

"Jerry, if I said that, I meant with the help of you and all of your people. The days of a consultant coming into a company, analyzing the problems, coming up with all of the answers, implementing solutions, and riding away into the sunset with the company staying on track and doing the things it needs to do to stay healthy are gone."

"Except in the minds of consultants, did those days ever exist at all?" asked Chuck.

"Well, a lot of consultants would have you believe so," answered Mike. "However, I've worked with middle-market companies like yours for my entire career. Middle-market companies have never had the money it takes to have consultants do the whole ball of wax," Mike continued. "The way I've always worked is something like a cross between a teacher and a coach. For example, one way to look at what we're going to do down here is that I'm going to train all of you to become your own consultants."

"Ohhh, cool," exclaimed Amy. "Does that mean we can go shopping for $1,000 suits while we're down here?"

"Amy, the only $1,000 suits you're going to find here are dive suits," replied Mike with a laugh. "No, what I meant was that no one in this group, myself and Jerry included, know enough to fix Cleveland Electronics all by themselves. So, we all have to work together in identifying issues and developing solutions. Furthermore, since proper implementation of the 'fixes' is the most important, time consuming, and therefore most expensive part of the consulting process, **you are going to be doing most of that work yourselves.**"

"With your help, of course."

"Yes with my help," replied Mike. "Because without the same kind of planning and execution that Cleveland Electronics needs in its business processes, this turnaround effort we are undertaking is bound to fail. In order to prevent that, I've developed certain methods over the years that establish accountability and motivate progress. You'll see what I mean as we get further into our work."

> "Because without the same kind of planning and execution that Cleveland Electronics needs in its business processes, this turnaround effort we are undertaking is bound to fail."

"So, Mike, it's almost like a circle then. Without focus and discipline, my company goes nowhere. But it takes focus and discipline to build infrastructure?"

"Right," said Mike with a grin. "An almost impossible problem—some people call it a '**CONUNDRUM**'."

"Mike, it almost seems like you're going to run our consulting project the same way that you're encouraging us to run Cleveland Electronics," said Jerry.

"Yes." replied Mike. "Because without the same kind of planning and execution that Cleveland Electronics needs in its business processes, this turnaround effort we are undertaking is bound to fail. In order to prevent that, I've developed certain methods over the years that establish accountability and motivate progress. You'll see what I mean as we get further into our work."

"So you're going to run our consulting project the same way that Cleveland Electronics will be running after you leave," said Jerry.

"Exactly," replied Mike. "Remember what I said about **continuous, focused action over time**? That concept applies to running a consulting engagement or any other kind of a long-term project just as much as it does to running a company. In fact, a big advantage to the methods we're going to use is that these methods are directly transferable to running your company."

"Will you explain that a little more, Mike?" asked Chuck.

"Sure. The short explanation is that, as we get toward the end of fixing the company, I'll start backing out of the process. Jerry or one of you will gradually take over as the project leader. Once all solutions have been implemented and the project ends, you'll find that the process I'm going to teach you can be used to implement and execute Cleveland Electronics' annual and strategic plans on an ongoing basis. In effect, the process itself becomes another form of infrastructure which is used to keep the company on-track."

> "…the process itself becomes another form of infrastructure which is used to keep the company on-track."

Mike and his clients spent another hour discussing the weather, the Keys, and where to go for dinner. After settling on the seafood buffet at Whale Harbor as the dining choice, the group walked to their cars for the drive to the restaurant.

*   *   *

Later that evening. The group had just finished dinner and was walking around the charter boats parked outside the restaurant. They were discussing what a great meal they'd just had, and what a warm, beautiful night they were in the process of experiencing.

"Except for that fish smell," exclaimed Amy.

"Nothing like the smell of sport fishing boats freshly washed and just off of the water," exclaimed Mike.

"Mike, have you ever dreamed of being a fishing boat captain?" asked Amy.

"I've thought about it, but I wouldn't say I've dreamed about it," replied Mike.

"I'm surprised that fishing all day on the water wouldn't be in your dreams," said Amy.

"Amy," Mike replied, "Most of these guys aren't making enough money to have the kind of lifestyle I'd like to have. Most of them are in it because they love to fish, and are willing to accept a lot of hard work and less than ideal conditions in other areas of their life in order to spend a lot of time on the water."

"But with all you know about business, couldn't you figure out a way to make money and spend all the time you want to on the water?" asked Amy.

"Amy," asked Mike, "what did I say were the two things every successful company must have?"

"Planning and execution?"

"Precisely. And in the sport fishing business, planning and execution add up to a great deal of hard work," replied Mike. "In other words, I love fishing. But I don't want to take one of my pastimes and turn it into hard work, which is what it'd be if I tried to make a living at it."

"That's easy enough to understand," said Chuck. "Do any of these guys make money?"

"As I said, very few are in the <u>business</u> of sport fishing. In fact, see the guy wiping down that boat over there? Let's go over and talk to him."

With that, the group approached the captain and owner of WIFE OUT. According to the sign over her slip, WIFE OUT is a 42-ft. Bertram

Sportsfisherman. Nick Baldwin, who has been fishing the Keys for marlin, sailfish, tuna, kingfish and other species for over 30 years, captains her. After introducing them and engaging in some warm-up chitchat, Dave finally asked:

"Nick, what kind of money can someone make in a business like this?"

"What are you, some kind of bean-counter?" asked Nick.

"Well…yes…that's exactly what I do," stammered Dave.

"Figures. That's exactly the kind of question I get from my bean-counter customers," chuckled Nick, throwing a knowing wink to the rest of the group. "Well, I'll tell you, if you want to make a lot of money, better stay up North and inject plastic into molds, or assemble auto parts, or make widgets, or do whatever the hell else it is you do up there. Because you don't make a lot of money in the charter fishing business."

"Then why are you in it?" asked Amy.

"Ever heard of quality of life?" asked Nick. "Because that's my primary motivation. Out on the ocean the air's pure, the smell of salt water's fine, and on the best days, the fish are biting. But even if they're not, I love being out on that water."

"And being out on the water in a $600,000 boat doesn't hurt either, I'll bet" said Mike.

"Oh, you're right," said Nick. "The boat's a big factor, too."

"Does your wife ever go with you on your charters?" asked Amy.

"I'm not married," said Nick. "I was married once, but then I saw this bigger boat. Couldn't afford both, so…."

"Ah, ha," laughed Amy. "And that's how you came up with the boat name!"

The rest of the group laughed while Nick turned a pale shade of red.

Mike broke in: "Nick, we've got to get going. The class here is going for an early start tomorrow morning. Tell you what, though. If we have any free time while we're down here, we'll give you a call and charter the WIFE OUT for an afternoon, fair enough?"

"Sure," replied Nick. "Take one of these cards and give me a call, anytime."

"Thanks, Nick," the group sang out as they headed to the cars for the drive back.

Chapter 22

8:00 AM the next morning, the Marathon Holiday Inn conference room.

Everyone was present, bright eyed, and bushy-tailed. After spending the first five minutes congratulating each other about how good they looked for this early in the morning, the topic swung around to the business at hand.

"Mike," said Jerry, "can you just kind of 'fast-forward' the retreat for us and explain exactly how and what we're about to do is going to fix the company?"

"Jerry, I must have answered that question at least three different times already," said Mike. "Now you want me to explain it again?"

Dave said, "I think it would be a good idea for all of us to hear this. Jerry and Mike have had a lot of time to talk about fixing the company without the whole team being present for the discussions. Last night before I fell asleep, I found myself wondering how it all comes together. I'd sure like to know a little more before we get into the nuts and bolts of guiding principles, core values, and all the rest of it."

"All right, gentlemen and lady," exclaimed Mike. "I'll try to explain it another way. Give me a moment to write on the board."

When Mike was finished, the white board at the front of the conference room looked liked this:

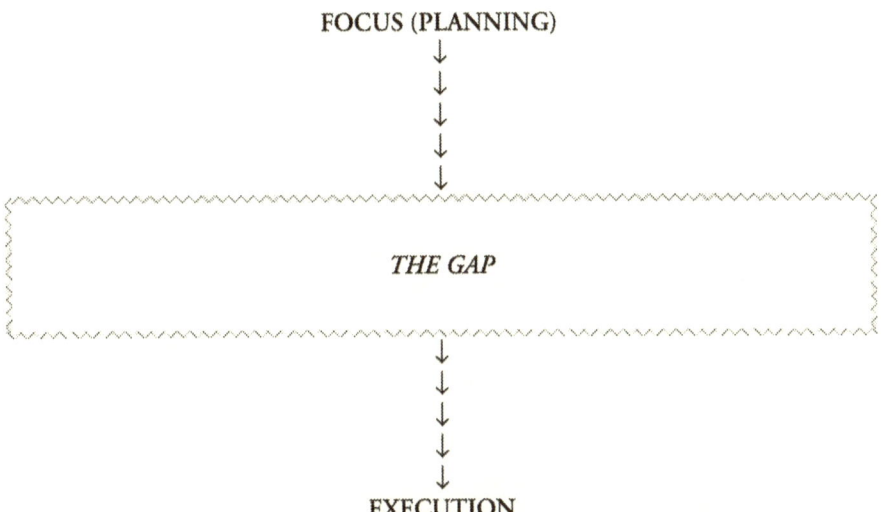

FOCUS (PLANNING)

THE GAP

EXECUTION

"All right, genius," said Jerry. "One thing is very obvious from what you've just written, Mike."

"And what's that, Jerry?"

"That you're a much better fisherman than you are an artist!" chimed in Chuck.

"Just what I was going to say," said Jerry. "Now, Mike, would you mind explaining your hieroglyphics, please?"

"Sure. The short explanation is that, as we get toward the end of fixing the company, I'll start backing out of the process. Jerry or one of you will gradually take over as the project leader. Once all solutions have been implemented and the project ends, you'll find that the process I'm going to teach you can be used to implement and execute Cleveland Electronics' annual and strategic plans on an ongoing basis. In effect, the process itself becomes another form of infrastructure which is used to keep the company on-track."

> **"…the process itself becomes another form of infrastructure which is used to keep the company on-track."**

"All right. Two important elements of a successful company are focus and good execution. Most companies start to develop focus by planning, strategic or otherwise. If a company can come up with a good plan…"

"Which starts to develop focus…" interjected Dave,

"And can do a good job of executing that plan…" continued Amy,

"Then that company will be successful and profitable." finished Jerry.

"YES!" Mike exclaimed. "My God, I think you've got it!"

"But just in case you don't get it, let me draw another chart." Mike then put this on the white board on the side of the room:

PLANNING	EXECUTION	EFFECT ON COMPANY
BAD	BAD	No profits
GOOD	BAD	No profits
BAD	GOOD	Minimal profits
GOOD	GOOD	High profits

"Well, this part's pretty self-explanatory," said Jerry. "But, let's go back to the chart at the front of the room for a sec. Just what do you mean by 'The Gap'?"

"OK, Jerry," replied Mike. "This part requires some explanation. For quite some time now, people who work with companies (all sizes of companies, by the way), have been observing that, while a whole lot of planning goes on in the business environment, many, if not most, of these plans don't get implemented. And even if plans get implemented initially, much, if not most, of the time the implementation falls apart down the road. With the result that a whole lot of the time, a company's plans get no further than the paper they are written on. And the best of plans do no good unless they are…*Class?*"

> "…a whole lot of the time, a company's plans get no further than the paper they are written on."

"**Implemented!**" shouted Jerry, Amy, Chuck and Dave.

"Right again!" said Mike in a pleased tone. "So, what we have is a GAP between a company's planed results and their actual results. And crossing that gap is what this retreat and the follow up work we are going to do is all about."

"I don't see how the Business Growth Model you had us working on fits in," said Jerry.

"Give me a minute," replied Mike. "Now, class, how do you suppose we can close the GAP for Cleveland Electronics?"

Amy threw out, "Wouldn't one way be to *communicate* the company's plans and strategies?"

"Yep," said Mike.

Chuck chimed in, "You'd also have to break the plans down into goals, policies and action steps as they affect each individual division, department, and employee."

"Right again," said Mike.

"And, you'd have to provide training to management and to employees so that they'd know **how to execute their part of the plans**," continued Jerry.

"Boy, you guys are on fire this morning," said Mike. "Must be high-test caffeine in that coffee you all are drinking."

Dave said. "And, of course, there needs to be accountability over the whole process so that everyone knows whether plans, policies, procedures and action steps are being accomplished."

> "…there needs to be accountability over the whole process so that everyone knows whether plans, policies, procedures and action steps are being accomplished."

"Dave, tell me more about that," said Mike. "What do you mean by 'accountability'?"

"Yeah," interjected Jerry. "I'd like to hear more about that, too. I've always thought our books, ledgers, financial statements and so on were very good—ever since I hired you four years ago, Dave."

"The kind of accountability I'm talking about has to do with people, not dollars," replied Dave. "I think that somehow, in the world of business that all of us have grown up in, the word **Accounting** has come to have a different meaning than the word **Accountability**, even though both words have the same root."

"You're on the right track, Dave," said Mike encouragingly.

Dave continued, "For some reason, **Accounting** has come to be associated with keeping track of the numbers, while **Accountability** implies that people are being held to things they commit to doing."

"Exactly right," said Mike. "And which comes first in the typical business process?"

"**Accountability**," the team chimed in.

"That's right, class," said Mike.

"OK, Mike," interjected Jerry, "but you still haven't answered the question of how the Business Growth Model fits in."

"We're almost there, Jerry," said Chuck. "Mike, can I finish the picture for him?"

"Go ahead, Chuck."

"Fine. All of the things we've just covered—plans, goals, policies, action steps, accountability—are part of a company's **infrastructure**. And **infrastructure** is what Mike's Business Growth Model is all about."

> "...**plans, goals, policies, action steps, accountability**—are part of a Company's infrastructure. And infrastructure is what Mike's **Business Growth Model is all about**."

"Bingo!" said Mike. And by looking at the faces of the others in the room, Mike could tell that they got it, too. "Jerry?" Mike queried.

"Yep, I've got it. It just became crystal clear," replied Jerry.

"How about the rest of you?" asked Mike.

The nods, affirmative statements, and overall mood of the team members indicated that, in fact, they got it. Cleveland Electronics had been suffering from a breakdown of infrastructure, which resulted in the company's inability to define and execute the plans it needed in order to become a profitable company and meet the other expectations that Jerry as the owner laid out. The Business Growth Model is a useful tool designed to point out the holes in Cleveland Electronics' infrastructure. Once these 'holes' are identified, Mike and the management team will develop action steps and accountabilities designed to fix the holes. And finally, Mike and Jerry will install a system of follow up to insure action steps are completed and new holes are identified and dealt with appropriately as the company moves forward.

By the time the above discussion was about to draw to a close, it was almost time for a break.

"So, in summary folks," said Mike, here's the rest of what we'll be doing to fix your company:

1) Identify 'holes'
2) Develop action steps and accountabilities, and
3) Implement"

"Of course," said Mike, "most of Step 3 will be done once we get back to Cleveland. Now, does anyone have any questions?"

"How long is our break?" asked Jerry.

"How about twenty minutes?" replied Mike.

With that, the team stood up, stretched, and took off to enjoy their break.

Chapter 23

A few minutes later. Dave Kork went out on the patio adjoining the Holiday Inn conference room. He was just about on his second gulp of fresh sea air when he noticed Jerry across the way, over by the pool bar. At this early hour of the morning, the bar was empty. Jerry had his cell phone out and was furtively punching in a number from a slip of paper. Dave noticed that something about Jerry's face wasn't normal. He wondered…wondered…then it hit him. The look was the same look Jerry had last year when it was time to determine Christmas bonuses. Jerry had just declared himself a large bonus in order to pay for a recent home-remodeling project. However, when it came to the employees, well, the money just wasn't there. Dave and Jerry discussed the situation at length before deciding on minimal bonuses for that year.

"Yeahhh," thought Dave, *"he's got that same guilty expression as when we decided bonuses last year. I wonder what the boss is up to?"*

Jerry finished the call and looked up with a start when he saw Dave looking at him from across the lobby. Heads nodded in acknowledgment, and both started making their way back to the meeting room.

Five minutes later, Mike recalled the meeting to order.

"OK, folks, let's get back to our formal agenda."

"Wait a minute, Mike, I didn't bring my tuxedo," cracked Jerry.

"Not a problem, Jerry. Here in Marathon the dress is 'Keys Formal' all the way."

"What in the world is Keys Formal?" Asked Amy.

"Well Amy, you know how everyone down here walks around in T-shirts with outrageous sayings on them and shorts?"

"Yep."

"Well, in Keys Formal, the saying on the T-shirt has no four letter words, and the shorts have no holes in them."

"Oh..." said Amy.

"Right. Well. Let's get going, shall we?" declared Chuck impatiently.

"Right now, my man," replied Mike. "Now, let's spend an hour and go over the things we did back in Cleveland in preparation for this session."

With that, Mike and the crew went over a lot of what had occupied their time over the past few weeks: defining the business that the company was in, the mission statement, the vision statement, and the company's core values. Because the team had spent a lot of time developing and discussing core values back home, the discussion didn't last very long. Before moving on to break new ground, Mike asked: "Does everyone see the value of doing these things: defining your business, mission statement, vision statement, core values, guiding principles?"

"I think its clear to us now, Mike," said Chuck. "All of these things have to do with Cleveland Electronics' infrastructure. Even though these things don't do much good by themselves, they are the building blocks to develop the planning and systems that we'll need in order to move the company forward."

"Chuck, I couldn't have said it better myself," said Mike.

Jerry jumped in. "You can compare a company's infrastructure to the infrastructure of a small town. Although the plan of where the roads, alleyways, etc. by itself doesn't do a bit of good, the plan is absolutely necessary if the finished infrastructure is going to meet the expectations of everyone in the town."

"That's right," said Mike.

"And, by the way, most towns and cities have a very active planning structure in place for just that reason," said Dave, who was on the planning and zoning board of the suburb where he lived.

"All right. On to the next step," said Mike. "Everyone, please pull out your 'Ten Point Planning Process' slides:

Ten Point Planning Process
1) Determine mission/vision/core values/guiding principles

2) Define the business you are in

3) **Set growth goals: Phase I, Phase II, Phase III**

4) Determine key jobs and get the right people in them. Define the management team.

5) Determine what is needed to get harmony in the management team and/or family

6) Define manager accountability

7) Set financial goals to get a balance among:

   -Profit

   -Cash flow

   -Equity

8) Identify core systems and determine what is needed to make them work

9) Identify industry trends and set product goals (stars and cash cows)

10) Create action plans: Assign responsibilities, budgets and target dates

"Now," continued Mike, "we've just spent the last hour going through steps 1 and 2 of the process, so now its on to Step 3. Have you discussed growth goals at your company in the past?"

Jerry and the management team spent the next 20 minutes discussing the past growth goals the company had had. It seemed as if the history of goals at Cleveland Electronics was a lot like that of other entrepreneurial oriented companies. For the first several years, ownership was so busy dealing with the day to day business that there was no time to think about goals. Oh, sure, there were always dreams: dreams of Mercedes, Lexus, small farms in Europe, yachts, and a house in Hawaii. The usual. But things were so busy that ownership put these things off to "some day." These kinds of dreams never became a part of the company's planning and therefore its infrastructure. As the discussion continued, Cleveland Electronics' management team, not surprisingly, decided that in the long term profitability was more important than sales. This was a foreseeable turn in the discussion, since many companies having problems showing a profit will make that their number one goal. After profitability was crowned "number one," the discussion next turned to "quality of life."

Jerry exclaimed "I'd just like to stop feeling like I'm a prisoner in my own company!"

Dave said, "And I'd like to stop running around with a lump at the bottom of my stomach wondering when the banker is going to call to tell me about our next unexpected overdraft."

Chuck remarked, "And I'd like to stop feeling like the main purpose of the sales force is to give me a heart attack by saving up major surprises impacting the production schedule until the last minute."

And finally Amy added, "I'd like to feel like I'm not the dispatcher at the Fire Department, always calling you folks and others to help us put out the next fire."

"So, guys," said Mike, "in terms of the Business Growth Model, it sounds like you'd like your growth goal to be successful negotiation of your crisis points in order to become a **Phase Three** company.

The team agreed that this was their goal. After a little more discussion and drawing on the white board, they found themselves looking at the following diagram:

Phase III Infrastructure

Consists of:

-Organization

-Planning

-Systems

Phase III Infrastructure

Guarantees:

-Owner freedom

-Continuity of earnings

-Good people with the ability to <u>develop</u> and <u>execute</u> critical long-term plans

"In other words," said Amy, "Phase III infrastructure closes the Gap between planning and execution."

"Right," replied Jerry. "Just like we were talking about before the break."

"All right, crew," said Mike, "it looks like we're now through with Step 3 of the Planning Process. Would anyone like to break for lunch?"

"Lunch sounds good," replied Chuck.

"Then it's to the cars, folks," said Mike. "We'll head over to Porky's for a quick sandwich. Then, I've got a real treat for you."

Chapter 24

Mike, Jerry, Amy, Chuck and Dave had a quick sandwich over at Porky's, a really "Keysey" place located on the Gulf of Mexico in Marathon. After lunch, they took a short walk over to a row of charter boats located right next door to Porky's.

Jerry struck up a conversation with a well-dressed gentleman standing on the dock looking at the boats.

"Going fishing this afternoon?" inquired Jerry?

"No, I'm afraid not," replied the gentleman.

"It looks like you want to, though," said Jerry.

"Well, I'd like to," the gentleman replied, "but I don't really have the time."

"Yeah, that's the story of my life, too," said Jerry. "Owning a business really keeps me busy."

"Yeah, me too," said the gentleman.

"Oh, so you own your own company?" asked Jerry.

"Yep."

"Where?"

"Down here."

"Nice," replied Jerry. "What kind of business are you in?"

"Oh, I own this business."

"What, the charter boats?"

"Yep," replied the gentleman.

"That's weird," said Jerry. "You see that portly balding guy over there?" Jerry pointed to Mike.

"Yep."

"He said you can't make any money in the charter fishing business. Said most guys do it for the love of fishing and being on the ocean, but that they don't make any money at it."

"Well," said the gentleman. "Did that guy charge you a lot of money to tell you that?"

"How did you guess?" asked Jerry incredulously.

"Because that sounds like something a consultant would say," smirked the gentleman.

"Well, mister, that's exactly what he is," said Jerry. "So, my expensive consultant is wrong?" he asked, suspiciously.

"Not at all," said the gentleman. "As with most things consultants say, he's partly right and partly wrong."

Amy had been listening in to the conversation.

"Now you've got me interested," said Amy. "What do you mean by partly right and partly wrong?"

"OK," said the gentleman, "let me explain. By the way, my name's Bob."

"Hi, Bob," said the group. For by now, they had all gathered around Amy and Jerry to try to catch a whiff of what was going on.

Bob began his story.

"You see, most people who get into this business do it for the love of fishing, the ocean, boats, you name it. They have a passion for the sea. I, on the other hand, never really liked boats. In fact, I tend to get sea-sick just looking at these boats sitting here tied to the dock."

"Then why'd you get into this business?" asked Amy.

"To make money," replied Bob. "You see, I had a successful manufacturing company up North for 30 years before I got down here five years ago. While running the manufacturing company, I found out what it takes to have a successful business. And when I sold the manufacturing company and moved down here, I wanted to see if my basic business principles could be used to start up and grow another successful business, but on a much smaller scale."

"And how's the 'experiment' going?" asked Jerry.

"We make a lot of money," said Bob.

"How do you do that?" said Dave.

"Well, there's a lot of things," said Bob. "But the main thing to keep in mind is **Focus.**"

"Uh, oh," said Amy. "I smell something fishy, and it isn't just the smell coming from those boats."

Just then, Mike walked up. "Aha," said Mike. "I see you've just met my friend Bob."

"We should have known," Chuck said to Mike. "Don't tell me. Bob was a client of yours when he had the manufacturing company, which you helped him turn around, which he then sold for millions of dollars before he ended up coming down here to the Keys."

"Chuck, that would make a lovely story if it were true," said Mike. "But no, the truth is, I met Bob a few years ago while I was having a sandwich at Porky's. Over the years, we've talked a lot about business back and forth. The reason we sound so much alike is that I think our ideas have just sort of 'cross-pollinated' with one another."

Dave asked, "Bob, can you tell us how your charter business is different from most of the other ones around here?"

"Well, for one thing, look at my boats," said Bob.

Amy said, "Yes, the first thing I noticed is that you have four boats here, all under the same business name."

"Right. The first thing that became apparent when I studied this business from the standpoint of making money is that you have to do sales and marketing in order to get customers. Most of the other charters just rely on word of mouth and a sign on their dock. Doing a good job of sales and marketing is very costly. Too costly for an operation with just one boat."

"I see," said Dave. "I also notice that your boats aren't very fancy. They've only got one engine, for example."

"Right again," said Bob. "Now, most of these charter guys who are doing it for the love of boats and fishing tend to have big, fancy boats."

Dave and the others thought back to their talk with Captain Nick the other night. *"Yeah, he's right about that,"* Dave thought.

"And those big fancy boats can cost anywhere from $250,000 to $700,000 new," continued Bob. "Plus, the bigger and fancier the boat, the higher the fuel, maintenance, insurance, dockage, and other costs. I keep my capital costs and operating costs low by staying with safe clean, plain boats that I buy used for a very good price. On average, about $82,000 a boat for the ones you see here. As a result my boat costs run about a third of the costs of the other guys."

"That sounds like a winning formula," said Dave. "What about your customers, though? Don't they like the luxury the other charter boats offer?"

"Ah, that's one of the ways **Focus** comes into play," said Bob.

"How's that?"

"Well, most of the fishermen who are our customers are average guys. Money's important to them. The big fancy boats need to charge $650 to $850 a day. With my lower costs, I can charge a couple hundred or so a day less, and make 'way more money than the fancy guys," chuckled Bob.

Mike chimed in. "Yes, and Bob's sales and marketing programs feature this lower price to bring in the business."

Jerry exclaimed, "You know Bob, it sounds like I can use some of your ideas in running my company."

"Sure," replied Bob. "Remember, I first learned some of this stuff running my manufacturing business."

Amy asked, "Bob, what other ways do you use FOCUS in your business?"

"That's easy. The first thing to remember is that a company can't achieve FOCUS without discipline. So, I run this business just like I ran my manufacturing plant, which was just like I ran my platoon in the Army. Focus and discipline come together on the things that are important to my customers and to the business."

> "The first thing to remember is that a company can't achieve FOCUS without discipline."

"For example, my customers like to catch fish, they like their boats clean, and they want to go out and come back on time and in a safe manner. So, in addition to hiring good captains and emphasizing these things to them, my policies and procedures provide that the captain cleans the boat immediately upon return from each trip; that the captain shows up at least a half hour before the trip goes out; and that my office person calls each captain an hour before the trip is scheduled to go out to insure the captain will show up. If the captain doesn't answer the call, the office person immediately contacts the back up captain, who takes the trip for that day."

"I'm impressed," said Chuck. "But how does discipline help in catching fish?"

"It helps in a lot of ways," continued Bob. "For one thing, I use a checklist in interviewing captains. I also have my other captains interview new captains. This helps me in attracting the kind of captains who have proven to be good fish catchers in the past. Also, one of the extra expenses I do allow myself is a subscription to an ocean temperature satellite service. The second thing the office person does after calling the captains every morning is to download an ocean chart. This chart shows the water temperatures in each of our fishing areas. Since temperature is one of the keys to finding fish, these charts drastically reduce the guesswork my captains have to do in order to find fish. Discipline insures that the chart is available to the captains before they start their trips for the day, and discipline requires that the captains use the chart rather than rely on guesswork. We also impart discipline to the guests on the boat. Before each vessel leaves the dock, the guests receive a safety briefing. In addition to telling them where the life jackets and head are located, the captain goes over various things that are important to the customer's enjoyment of the trip. Of course, the briefing outline is printed on a laminated card, and we require that the captain refer to the card in doing his briefing."

"Another very important contribution to discipline is what I do on a daily basis," continued Bob.

"Let me guess." chimed in Dave. "You provide accountability for the boat captains and other employees?"

"Right you are," beamed Bob. "I can tell that Mike Henderson has had an influence on you. Dave, you are one hundred percent correct. By enforcing the company's rules and procedures, each of my employees feels accountable—not only to me, but to the customers and to the other employees as well. And this accountability results in more satisfied customers, more satisfied employees, and a fat bank account."

> **"By enforcing the Company's rules and procedures, each of my employees feels accountable…"**

"Bob, you've been more than kind in sharing your story with us," beamed Jerry. "But now we need to be getting back to work. We're going to be talking about applying some of these things to my company as well."

"Jerry, if you folks decide you're working too hard and need a break, my brochures are all over that Holiday Inn you're meeting at. I'd love to take you out for a day's fishing and show you how all of this works in practice."

"That sounds like a great idea," said Amy. "Hopefully, we'll be able to work that out."

With that, the crew loaded the car and drove back to the Holiday Inn.

Chapter 25

Back at the meeting room. Mike said, "All right. Look at your *Ten Point Planning Process* again. Let's look at steps 4, 5 and 6:"

Ten Point Planning Process

1) Determine mission/vision/core values/guiding principles

2) Define the business you are in

3) Set growth goals: Phase I, Phase II, Phase III

4) **Determine key jobs and get the right people in them. Define the management team.**

5) **Determine what is needed to get harmony in the management team and/or family**

6) **Define manager accountability**

7) Set financial goals to get a balance among:

   -Profit

   -Cash flow

   -Equity

8) Identify core systems and determine what is needed to make them work

9) Identify industry trends and set product goals (stars and cash cows)

10) Create action plans: Assign responsibilities, budgets and target dates

Mike continued, "It makes sense to discuss these three steps together, because they all have to do with the management team. And, most importantly, Phase II companies like yours tend to do things in certain ways that get in the way of successful completion of these three steps. Amy, can you think of anything that Cleveland Electronics or its people do that would prevent the company from doing one or more of these steps?"

"Mike, is it my imagination, or do you pick on me by asking me the most difficult questions?" asked Amy.

"I hope I'm not picking on you, Amy," replied Henderson. "But just to make sure, from now on I'm keeping track of the questions I'll be asking each of you throughout the session."

"Well," Amy continued, "I do see something. In Step 6 you talk about defining manager accountability. It seems like we don't have anyone in the company who is accountable to other managers. Everyone just comes running to Jerry. Is that what you mean by something that would prevent us from accomplishing these steps?"

"Amy, that's exactly what I'm talking about," said Mike. "And, that's exactly why I ask you so many hard questions. You seem to have the correct answers."

Amy blushed.

"But isn't that how small companies are supposed to work?" asked Jerry. "I mean, I don't want us to get bogged down in the bureaucracy I had at the large company I worked for before starting Cleveland Electronics."

"Valid point, Jerry," said Mike. "And, in fact, that is how small companies work. But in order for a small company to grow into a big company, its management structure has to change. Here, let me draw a picture of your current organization chart:"

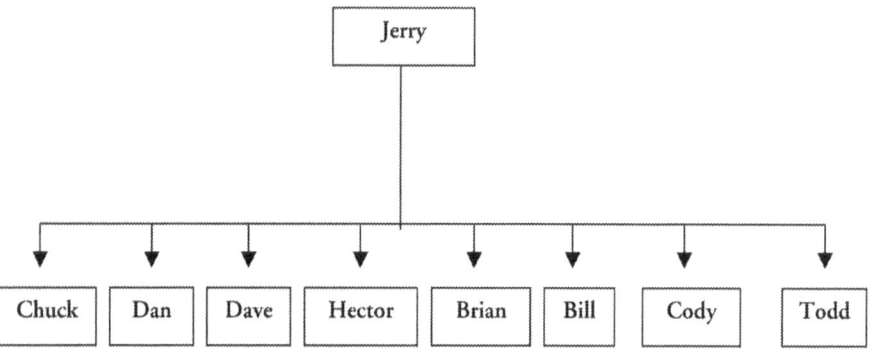

Dave observed, "That drawing kind of looks like a rake."

"Terrific observation, Dave!" exclaimed Mike. "Because that's just what we call this kind of a management structure—**Rake Management**. And it's typical of Phase I and Phase II Companies."

"You mean we're not unique?" commented Chuck dryly.

"Not at all," said Mike. "In fact, the basic driver of this kind of a management style is…"

"Wait, wait, let me guess," said Jerry. "The main reason you find this kind of a structure in smaller companies is the owner's need to control everything?"

"You've hit the nail right on the head, Jerry," replied Mike. "You see, with a rake management structure, all the important mangers in the company report directly to the owner. The owner's in control. Nothing can happen without his or her direct input. But, can someone give me the drawbacks to this kind of a structure?"

Chuck replied, "It seems to me that the company can only get so big before this kind of a structure starts to choke the company. In fact, the more I think about it, I see that this is one of the things that has been choking our company for at least the past two years. When real problems come up, I can only do so much to try and resolve them before I have to go to Jerry in order to finish the resolution of the issue."

Amy added, "As the person who's in charge of always rushing to find Jerry to finish putting out fires, Chuck, I'd have to say you're right."

Chuck again. "Yeah. Come to think about it, the last couple of fires we've had to put out were really caused by the inability of my department heads to act without going to Jerry or to myself for a decision."

"Are you referring to that incident over the 240 A PC board and whether it could be substituted for the 312 V last week?" asked Jerry.

"That's one incident," replied Chuck. "The other one was whether to go with Nalcotron or Chemserv as our primary solvent supplier." I think that what we're getting at is that these kinds of decisions should be made at the lowest possible level, without everyone running to you all of the time for a decision."

"Right," said Mike.

And from Dave, "Mike, I think we're all on the same page here. But how do you fix it? Is this as easy as just coming up with a new organization chart?"

"Not at all," replied Mike. "But I think you knew that. When we leave this session, we'll have as a follow up item the need to redraw the company's organization chart to enable further growth. But just doing that isn't enough. To answer Dave's question, the biggest barrier to implementing the new chart will be to get each of you to do things differently under the new structure. And the biggest hurdle there is going to be…"

> "…the biggest barrier to implementing the new chart will be to get each of you to do things differently under the new structure. And the biggest hurdle there is going to be to overcome the owner's fear of letting go…"

"To overcome the owner's fear of letting go," finished Jerry.

"Exactly right again, Jerry," replied Mike. "Isn't it funny how so many of the issues we face in business have to do with psychology?"

"Is that because so many of us business owners are crazy?" asked Jerry.

"Yes. Owners as well as people like me who try to work with them," said Mike with a short laugh. "And as long as we're on the subject, let's talk a little more about the kinds of people who make up Cleveland Electronics and its management team."

"Like most companies, Cleveland Electronics can be thought of as being made up of three kinds of people: Leaders, Managers and Technicians. And each of these types has very different personality characteristics and ways of looking at things. The key is to find ways to get these different people working together for the good of the company."

"Sounds like more psychology," said Jerry.

"Yes, but let's try to keep it practical," exclaimed Chuck.

"OK, Chuck," replied Mike. "If I get too far off the path, it's your job to pull me back to earth, agreed?"

"Right!" exclaimed Chuck.

"That way, everyone, if we end up getting lost in a sea of 'touchy feely' here, it's Chuck's fault, OK?"

"Absolutely!" everyone exclaimed with a laugh.

"OK, let's look at the characteristics of a leader," said Mike as he put this chart up on the wall:

Leader

- Visionary—focuses on future
- Empowers through intensity and commitment
- Inspirational to be around
- High level of commitment to products, services, concept of company
- Seems to be a risk-taker
- Knows personal limitation and achieves needed balance through other people—internal and external
- Sees the "big picture" of the company, the industry
- Trusts intuition and acts on it
- Strong market creator

"Can anyone doubt who we're talking about here?" asked Mike.

After a few minutes of discussion, everyone agreed that Jerry, as the leader of Cleveland Electronics, possessed all of the characteristics listed on the above chart.

"Now," said Mike as he put the following chart up on the wall, "let's take a look at the characteristics of a good manager:"

Manager

- Gets day-to-day work done through other people—effective delegator
- Coach/Teacher
- Low need to be liked—can deal with conflict
- Identifies with management
- Deadline oriented
- Operations oriented—focuses on present
- Attention to detail
- Methodical—systems oriented
- Takes strong responsibility for others
- Sees the "big picture" of the day-to-day jobs and how each relates to the other—assembles productive teams

"Now," said Chuck, "do any of you see yourselves in this chart?" Everyone nodded except Jerry.

"Mike," do you have another chart to show us?" asked Chuck.

"You bet I do," said Mike. "Let's take a look at the characteristics of a Technician:"

Technician

- Performs individually
- Learns one of a few skills well
- Identifies with the "workers"
- Strong responsibility for self
- Sees the "big picture" of own job
- Communicates clearly about job related issues
- Takes responsibility to develop needed skills for job. Operates best when in technical comfort zone

"Very, very interesting." exclaimed Chuck.

"Why so?" asked Mike.

"It seems like each of the three types are very different kinds of people," said Chuck. "I mean, look at the Leader. It says he is a visionary—always focused on the future. On the other hand, the Manager has to focus on day-to day tasks—getting these things done through other people, the chart says. And, look at the Technician—he or she identifies with the workers and has a strong sense of 'self". Big difference between the Technician and the Manager, who sees the big picture of things and has to focus on getting the job done through other people."

"And, what an even bigger difference between the Technician and the Leader," said Dave. "The Leader is focused on the big picture. The Technician focuses on his or her own job. And here's another big one—the Leader is a visionary and is focused on the big picture. The Manager is detail oriented, and focused on the day-to-day."

"Well, in my case," said Chuck, "I see myself in both the Manager and Technician profiles."

"How did you start your career, Chuck?" asked Mike.

"I started off as a tool maker," said Chuck. "Then I switched companies and took a job as a machine set-up man. Since then, I've had a few management jobs, but always on the factory side of the wall."

Amy said, "Well, then, Chuck, is it possible the 'old Chuck" is relating more to the Technician, and the 'new Chuck' to the Manager?"

"I think you might be right," replied Chuck.

Dave was impressed by how much of the technician was still in him, despite his attempts to become more of a manager. Dave saw that in order to be a better manager, he would have to overcome his love for detail and his high need to be liked, two traits common to good technicians, in order to perform more effectively on the company's management team.

For the next half-hour, Jerry, Mike and the others discussed the three charts and how they related to Cleveland Electronics. One of the first things that came up was the marked difference between the Leader and the Manager. Jerry realized that one of the reasons he felt bored sometimes is that he spent a lot of time **managing** rather than **leading**. And when all was said and done, Jerry realized that he was a far better **Leader** than he was a **Manager**. The group also noted that the Leader seemed to be very future-oriented. Chuck, remembering one of his past management seminars, remarked how nothing got done if all a company focused on was the future.

> "...nothing got done if all a company focused on was the future. Although a company might need to look at the past and the present, all relevant actions needed to move the company along take place in the now..."

"Although a company might need to look at the past and the present, all relevant actions needed to move the company along take place in the now, was how the seminar leader put it, I think," said Chuck.

"Right, Chuck," said Mike. "And remember our discussion about 'the Gap'? Maybe the reason the **Gap** exists is because planning is concerned with the past and the future while execution is all about the now-and people don't realize this?"

Jerry then remarked, "I just realized something. If I want to continue focusing on my vision for the company and how to get there, I'm really going to need you managers and our technicians to be focused on getting things done in the now, both to run our business and to help me carry out those action steps we need to move the company towards where I want it to be."

"I think we're all starting to see that more clearly," said Chuck.

"And while we're at it, we need to get all three of these diverse groups working together," commented Dave.

Mike answered, "Before we get into the solutions, let's summarize a little bit about the differences between the Leader, Manger, and Technician." For the next 15 minutes, the team worked on this. The following is the result of their work:

Leader-Manager-Technician
Comparison Chart

Leader	Manager	Technician
Works through other people	Works through other people	Performs individually
Focuses on future	Focuses on day-to-day	Focuses on day to day
Intense and committed to goals of the company	—-	Committed to doing own job well
Inspirational to be around	Low need to be liked	Need to be liked by peers
—	Takes responsibility for actions of others	Takes responsibility for self
Empowers through intensity and commitment	Methodical-systems oriented	Methodical-task oriented
Visionary—big picture of the company, industry, customers	Sees "big picture" of multiple jobs and how they relate	Sees "big picture" of own job
Seems to be a risk taker	Methodical-systems oriented	Low risk tolerance—operates best in technical comfort zone

Mike then asked, "All right, now, group, now that we've been through all of that, what do we need to do in order to get Cleveland Electronics on the right path?"

"It seems like the first thing we need to do is to redraw the organization chart, right?" asked Amy.

"As always, Amy, you're absolutely right," exclaimed Mike. "Does anyone have any ideas?"

"As a matter of fact, Mike, I've been drawing the start of our new chart as you all have been discussing other things," remarked Jerry.

"That's about what I figured," said Mike. "Well, Jerry, what have you come up with?"

"In order for the company to work better, we need a 'stacked' organization structure. Something where I have no more than three or four people reporting directly to me. Isn't that right, Mike?"

"You're right so far, Jerry. Three or four direct reports are about the right number according to the 'command and control' experts."

"'Command and control'? What's that?" asked Chuck suspiciously as he exercised his new additional duty as the team's 'touchy feely' police.

"Don't worry, Chuck, its not a psychological term," said Mike. "In fact, it's almost the exact opposite. It's a military term. As a matter of fact, a lot of modern business theory comes from the military model used to control large organizations in combat situations. When you come right down to it, a lot of the terms and concepts used in business today, like *strategy, execution, tactics*, etc. had their origins in the military."

"Oh, boy," exclaimed Jerry. "Here we go on the military stuff again."

"Nah, don't worry about that, Jerry," said Mike. "What we're about to get into is far too important for me to interrupt with war stories. I'll save those for tonight when we're sitting around having dinner."

"Well…er.." stammered Jerry.

"What, Jerry, are you going to be anti-social tonight?" asked Amy.

"Ah…no. Its just that I may have plans," said Jerry, haltingly. *"I need to find Amber and tell her that I want that coin,"* he thought.

"All right. Whatever," replied Mike. "Let's take a couple of minutes to stretch and then we'll get into solving our organizational problems. That should finish out the afternoon."

Chapter 26

When the session resumed, Jerry presented his idea of the company's new organization chart and the group worked on it. After some discussion, the team decided that the company should be organized along the following lines:

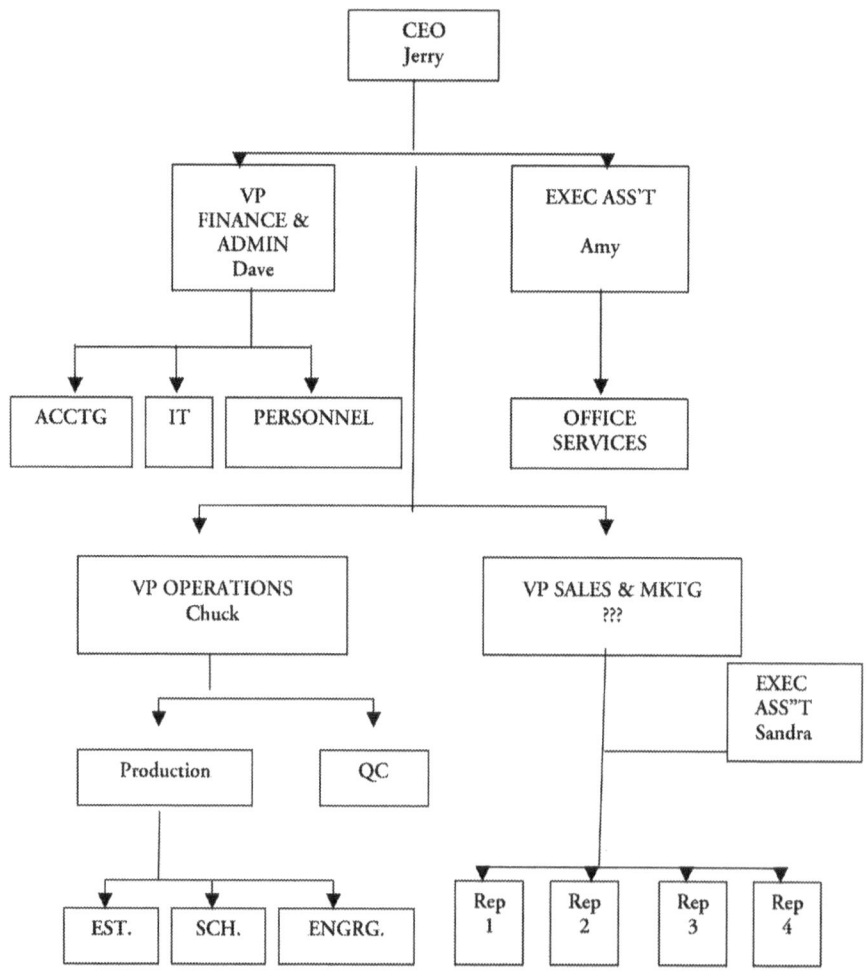

"You know, Mike," said Jerry, "we've had these kinds of organization charts in the past."

"In fact," Amy said, "remember about five or six years ago when we had that other consultant in? He helped us come up with something very similar to this chart."

"Ah, ha!" exclaimed Mike. "No wonder Jerry was able to come up with something so fast. Jerry, what happened to that organization chart?"

"Let me see," replied Jerry. "As I recall, we had it all typed up. We had a couple of meetings with the management and with the employees. We talked about it several times. And then, for some reason, it just faded away."

"Oh, Jerry," Amy said. "I'm remembering more now. What happened was that we were all getting used to the new structure, and everything seemed to be going well. Then we lost Cabletec as a customer, and a couple of weeks later we almost lost Ariscom. Remember?"

"I remember," said Dave. "At that time, Ariscom was our largest customer. We got scared, and our focus totally shifted towards replacing Cabletec's business and keeping Ariscom from sourcing their assemblies overseas."

"That's right," said Jerry. "We had to focus on those crises, and we forgot about the new organization structure."

Mike asked, "Did losing those customers have anything to do with the new organization chart?"

"No, not that I recall," said Jerry.

"Then why didn't you just meet those challenges using the new organization?" asked Mike.

The team talked about this for a while. Their stomachs were starting to growl as the hour slowly rolled towards 7:00 PM. Then Chuck observed, "Even though I wasn't here back then, it sounds to me like everyone just went back to doing what they were comfortable with."

"That's it exactly," said Amy. "Under pressure, we forgot about the new organization, and went back to what had worked in the past."

"Worked?" asked Mike. "Then why did you switch to the new organization in the first place?"

"Mike's right," said Jerry. "We went to the new organization because what we were doing wasn't working, and we realized it. Yet, after we solved our problem with a new structure, we threw it out the window when these two customer crises came along."

"Why do people do that?" asked Amy.

"Human nature," said Chuck. "Under pressure, most people will usually go back to old behavior, because the old behavior is more comfortable. Even if it doesn't work."

"There's got to be more to it than that," said Dave.

"There's a lot more to it than that," replied Mike. "But, in order to really explain it, we'd have to get into psychology, which we said we wouldn't do. So let's just leave it at Chuck's observation, and pick up here tomorrow morning."

Chapter 27

9:15 PM that evening. Mike, Jerry and the team were just finishing dinner at Odette's Steak and Lobster House, one of Mike's favorite restaurants.

"Mike, that was truly delicious," said Jerry. "I see why you like it here."

"Yeah, this is probably my favorite place in Marathon," replied Mike.

"How'd you ever find the place?" asked Chuck.

"That's an interesting story," replied Mike. "When I first started coming down to the Keys, I didn't really know that much about fishing in salt water, since all of my fishing had been around the Great Lakes and some of the farm ponds around where I was raised in Ohio. Odette's husband is one of the best charter-fishing captains around. I started fishing with him and he led me to the restaurant."

"Now, tell me, Mike, is Odette's husband one of the charter guys who doesn't make money because they love fishing, or does he run a real business like our friend Bob from this afternoon?" asked Dave.

"If you all are done with dinner, why don't we go into the bar and ask him?" suggested Mike.

"How do you know he's in there?" asked Jerry.

"Oh, he's in there, all right," said Mike. "Or else he's three blocks west of here, laid out in a casket at McClusky's funeral home."

With a short laugh, the group left the dining room and walked into the bar. Sitting in about the middle of the bar was an enormous balding man who was regaling the clientele with some slightly off-color jokes.

"Hi, Dick," greeted Mike.

"Why, hello, partner," said Dick. "Looks like you brought another load of tourists in. Pretty soon you'll have enough to retire on, what with all of the 'finder's fees' I'm paying' you."

"I wish," said Mike with a chuckle. "Dick, meet Jerry, Amy, Chuck, and Dave."

Hi, folks," said Dick. "What brings all of you to the Keys?"

"We're here doing a management workshop," replied Jerry.

"Oh. Wouldn't be interested in a little fishing, would you?" asked Dick hopefully.

"If mean old Mr. Mike would allow it, we'd love to get on the water for a couple of hours," replied Amy.

"Yeah, but we've got a lot of work to do in the next two days," said Jerry.

"Shame," said Dick. "You know, the dark of the moon is tonight, which means that tomorrow should bring some of the best mahi-mahi fishing of the season."

"Mahi-mahi? I thought you only caught those in Hawaii," said Dave.

"No," said Dick. "That's the new name for dolphin (the fish) that we're trying to use down here. Before when we talked about catching dolphin people got freaked out because they thought we were going after Flipper. A lot of people from up North don't know that Flipper was a mammal, and that there's also a dolphin fish that most folks see on a restaurant menu as Mahi-mahi."

"So I can't interest you in a fishing trip?" coaxed Dick.

"I'm afraid not this time," said Mike.

"Say, Dick," asked Jerry, "this is a huge restaurant. I'll bet you and Odette stay pretty busy running this place and trying to stay on top of the charter business as well."

"Well, it's a challenge sometimes," said Dick, "but we do pretty well at it. Well enough so that my lovely wife and I not only enjoy running both operations, but we manage to get out fishing together once or twice a week as well."

"Wow." said Amy. "That's a real accomplishment. How do you manage that?"

"Actually, said Dick, it started about the time that Mike started fishing with me. As I recall, he and I were out catching sailfish one day, and I was complaining about how running two businesses and trying to raise three kids was beating the hell out of Odette and me. We started talking about business management and how much organization has to do with running a business smoothly."

"Amazing," said Chuck. "We were just talking about the same topic before we came over here for dinner."

"Yeah, well, Mike and I got to talking and we decided that what Odette and I were really looking for was freedom without worry. When we started looking at things, it turned out that we had started to build a really nice organization, but we wouldn't let the people we had in management positions do their jobs."

> "...it turned out that we had started to build a really nice organization, but we wouldn't let the people we had in management positions do their jobs..."

"Can you give us an example?" inquired Amy.

"Well, for example, although we tried to hold the shift supervisors responsible for running the restaurant during their shift, Odette and I insisted on making all of the hiring and firing decisions. The employees knew this, and would try to do an 'end run' around the supervisors."

"So," said Amy, "what did you do?"

"Things got a lot better when we gave the shift supervisors hiring and firing authority," replied Dick. "As soon as we did that, the quality of service improved and the supervisors told us their jobs got a lot easier."

> "Things got a lot better when we gave the shift supervisors hiring and firing authority..."

Mike added, "A lot of business owners make the same mistake; they try to delegate responsibility without delegating authority."

The team just looked at one another; after a few seconds, Jerry, looking down at the floor, softly uttered one simple word: "Guilty."

"Whatever," announced Mike. "We'll talk more about this tomorrow. Why don't all of us pile in the car and get back to the hotel; we've got a long day ahead of us tomorrow."

"Sounds like a plan," said Dave. "I just have one more question for Dick."

"Shoot," said Dick.

> "A lot of business owners make the same mistake; they try to delegate responsibility without delegating authority."

"Who's the guy with the suit in the picture holding the long silver fish with black spots on its tail?" asked Dave, pointing to an eight-by-ten-inch picture hanging on the wall in the entryway to the bar.

"I'm glad you asked that question," said Dick. "The guy in the suit's my lawyer. After I took that shot, I emailed the picture to all of his friends with the caption 'Which one's the barracuda?' Really got the laughs here in town."

"Is he still working for you?" asked Amy.

"Come to think of it," said Dick, "I haven't heard from him in a while. Maybe I'll give him a call."

"Might be a good idea, Dick," said Mike as he ushered the team out of the restaurant and into the car for the trip back to the Holiday Inn.

Chapter 28

8:00 AM the next morning. Holiday Inn conference room. Mike and the crew were all assembled and raring to go.

Chuck opened with: "Hey, Mike, let's talk some more about what Dick mentioned in the bar last night. I've been thinking about what he said about hiring and firing authority and his organization. It seems to me that a big part of our problem here at Cleveland Electronics has been that we the management team are supposed to run our areas and deal with all of the problems, but we don't have the authority to do the things it takes to accomplish that. Every time we need to get a critical task done, like firing an unruly worker, for example, it seems like we need Jerry's approval."

"And another thing," said Dave. "Some of the factory supervisors have been complaining recently that their people are going above their heads—to you, Chuck, or to Jerry, for example, to get issues resolved. Mary the QC supervisor, for example, told me the other day that Jerry approved two days off for Carol, one of her employees, without her knowing about it."

"And," said Chuck, "Jerry's not the only one. Just the other day, I approved a modification to one of our assemblies for a customer without going through engineering. It just seemed like the expedient thing to do."

"All right," said Mike. "I think we all get the general idea. Now, its time for the first two rules that will govern our new organization structure:

Rule Number One	Follow the chain of command
Rule Number Two	Supervisors must have the right to evaluate, hire and fire their people."

The team talked at length about their two new rules. Rule Number One means that Jerry can no longer direct employees who are under another manager or supervisor. If Jerry, for example, sees a plant employee performing an operation incorrectly, Jerry needs to go to the employee's immediate supervisor or to the supervisor's manager to solve the problem. Additionally, the team decided that, although supervisors would be granted the authority to review, hire and fire their staff, they would do this under the direction of policies to be drafted and implemented by the personnel department.

"The chain of command sounds a lot like the Army," observed Amy.

"Oh, boy, here we go," smirked Jerry, who by now was used to Mike's war stories.

"That's because I got it from the Army," said Mike. "In the service, they also taught us two additional principles that are apropos:

—Never delegate responsibility without authority, and

—You can always delegate authority, but you can never delegate responsibility."

"Somebody help me here!" exclaimed Chuck. "Aren't those two statements contradictory?"

"In a certain way, they are," said Mike. "That's why I never just throw them out there. They take some explanation."

For the next ten minutes, Mike explained the two statements. In smaller organizations and sometimes even in larger ones, managers and supervisors will occasionally delegate responsibility but, due to fear of loss of control or other motivation, won't give the subordinate the authority they need to fulfill their accountabilities. For example, if an owner is going to hold the shop foreman responsible for the efficiency of the shop, the foreman must have the authority to hire, fire, discipline, evaluate and otherwise deal with the employees under him. Although the company may establish policies requiring review of these decisions with the owner or the human resource department, the shop foreman must be given this ultimate authority if his area of responsibility is to be run effectively. The second statement means that although a supervisor or manger delegates responsibility for an area to a subordinate, that supervisor or manager remains accountable for the performance of the subordinate's operating unit. Therefore, the delegating supervisor or manger must maintain oversight over the subordinate to insure the subordinate is doing the job correctly. Too often, untrained or inexperienced managers will simply "delegate and forget," sometimes with disastrous results.

Mike said, "Well, applying this last half hour of discussion to Cleveland Electronics should solve a lot of your problems right there."

Jerry interjected, "I agree. Shouldn't we write down the part about coming up with policies for hiring, firing and evaluating our employees so we don't forget about it?"

Mike replied, "Jerry, we're going to do something better than that before this crowd goes back to Cleveland; but for now, yes, why don't you just write that point down. We'll come back to it before we end the retreat."

"OK," said Jerry.

Mike then said, "Let's go back to the organization chart a minute. Are we sure we have the right people in the right jobs?"

"Let's start with the easy one first," replied Chuck. "We haven't had anyone in the VP-Sales position since Jason left."

"Right. We're going to need to fill that job pretty soon," said Jerry. "What kind of person are we going to need?"

"Tell you what, Jerry," said Mike. "Let's just put that one on your follow up list, too, OK?"

"Right," said Jerry. "It's done."

"Now," said Mike. "Does everyone here feel that they're in the right job?"

Everyone in the room thought about it, and looked at one another. After a few minutes of discussion, it seemed that everyone felt they were in the right slot on the chart, but that they were missing something.

"We'll ask you that one again later on in the process," said Mike. "After we're back in Cleveland and have done some detailed strategic and business planning, we'll revisit each of your roles in the 'new' company. When we do that, some of you might have a different opinion than you do now."

"Is there any more we need to do with the organization chart before we move on?" Jerry asked, somewhat impatiently.

"I don't know about you, but I sure could use some training in how to be a better manager," said Chuck.

"Good point," said Dave. "I could too. And what about the supervisors under us? I'll bet very few of them ever received any training or guidance on how to be an effective manager or supervisor."

The team again talked at length on this subject. After about 20 minutes, Mike again said, "Jerry, how about writing that down as a follow up item as well. 'Coming up with a program for training and development of management and supervisors.'"

"Got it," said Jerry. "Can we move on now?"

"How about it, team?" asked Mike.

The team agreed.

"Very good," replied Mike. "Will all of you please take out your "Ten Point Planning Process" slides.

For the next few minutes, they discussed the steps on the planning slides, and crossed off the steps they had completed. When they were finished, the slides looked like this:

Ten Point Planning Process

1) ~~Determine mission/vision/core values/guiding principles~~

2) ~~Define the business you are in~~

3) ~~Set growth goals: Phase I, Phase II, Phase III~~

4) ~~Determine key jobs and get the right people in them. Define the management team.~~

5) ~~Determine what is needed to get harmony in the management team and/or family~~

6) Define manager accountability

7) Set financial goals to get a balance among:

-Profit

-Cash flow

-Equity

8) Identify core systems and determine what is needed to make them work

9) Identify industry trends and set product goals (stars and cash cows)

10) Create action plans: Assign responsibilities, budgets and target dates

"It looks to me like we're about half way through," said Dave.

"Half way through with the Planning Process, maybe," said Jerry. "But don't forget, we've got to go through the items we circled on the Phase II slides as well."

"You're right," said Chuck. "But it looks like we've made good progress so far."

"As a matter of fact, folks," said Mike, "I'm cautiously optimistic that we'll get our work done tomorrow and still have time for some recreation before we have to go back to Cleveland."

The group met Mike's comment with great enthusiasm. On the momentum of Mike's comment, they swung right into Point # 6, above:

6) Define manager accountability

"There's that lovely word **Accountability** again," said Dave.

"Told you it was important," said Mike.

"Can you explain what this point means, Mike?" asked Amy.

"Why don't you try, Jerry?" asked Mike.

"OK. As we discussed yesterday, in order for a manager to feel responsible for his or her area, they have to be held accountable. In other words, you can't just tell someone what to do, or give them a responsibility, and expect them to carry it out. They have to be held accountable for results."

"Excellent," said Mike. "And the more detailed you can make the description of a manager's 'accountabilities,' the better."

"Or even an employee's accountabilities" interjected Dave.

"Right. Even an employee's."

"It sounds like we're heading towards job descriptions for every employee and manager in the company," remarked Amy.

"That's exactly where we're heading," said Mike. "And we can't possibly get those done in the time we have left. In fact, we probably couldn't even map out the key accountabilities for each one of your jobs," he continued.

"Then what do we do?" asked Amy.

"I know," said Jerry. "Let's ask for a volunteer, and map out their key accountabilities. Then, when we get back to town, we can do the rest of the managers and employees."

"Right Jerry," said Mike. "So on your follow up list, write down 'job descriptions, including accountabilities, for all employees, including managers. Now, who wants to volunteer to be our guinea pig?"

"I will," said Chuck.

"Good, Chuck, I was hoping you'd volunteer. You'll make an ideal example," said Mike enthusiastically. "Let's start out by having Chuck describe his job and what he's accountable for."

Chuck described his position as requested. When he was finished, various team members commented on whether Chuck's perceptions were the same as or differed from their own. As they were talking, Mike wrote on the white board. As the discussion progressed, Mike tried to get as much specificity as possible into the measurements of Chuck's accountabilities. When they were done, the board looked like this:

Accountabilities:

General:

Efficient operation of the plant
Quality of product
Well being of employees
Plant cleanliness and safety
Actively participate in general management of the company

Measurements:

Monthly plant efficiency calculations
Reject rates
Hours of time lost due to accidents

Satisfactory results on OSHA and other plant inspections
Achievement of overall profit objectives of company for the year

"That's excellent," said Mike. "Dave, can you explain to us what 'monthly plant efficiency calculations' are?"

Dave replied, "They show the overall efficiency of the plant, and include such things as direct labor as a percentage of sales, material cost as a percentage of sales, labor and materials cost variances, budgeted costs versus actual, and a few other items."

"Thanks, Dave," said Mike. "Did we leave anything out?"

"I think that about does it," replied Jerry.

The rest of the group agreed. They reiterated that, when they got back to Cleveland, they would begin to document accountabilities for all mangers and employees, and incorporate these into updated job descriptions. When the discussion waned, Jerry suggested a break, and the group stopped talking and headed for the door.

Chapter 29

Ten minutes later. The hotel lobby.

Jerry punched in Amber's number on his cell phone again. Still no answer. Jerry had tried and tried to call last night, but had no luck in getting through. When he thought about going to the restaurant to see if Amber might be working, he remembered that it was Monday night, and the place was closed. Jerry started to worry. *"Gee, if I don't hook up with her tonight, we've got only one more night down here. And with Mike's plans for an outing tomorrow, I might not have my chance tomorrow night."* Jerry took the paper with Amber's number on it out of his pocket. In studying the numbers, he realized that he might have made a mistake. The "6" on the paper might have been an "8." Sure enough, when he dialed again, he got Amber's answering machine.

"Hi. I'm not home right now, but if you leave a message, I'll try to get back to you as soon as possible. Goodbye for now."

Jerry left a message that emphasized that he wanted to purchase the silver Cobb coin, but that he might be in town only through tonight. He left his cell phone and hotel number for Amber to call back. He resolved to visit the restaurant tomorrow night if he didn't hear back from Amber before then. When he closed his cell phone, he looked up and noticed Dave and Chuck watching from across the lobby. Jerry smiled, waved, and ducked back into the meeting room.

Dave and Chuck noticed Jerry look up and glance across the lobby. They returned his wave, and looked at each other as Jerry darted back into the meeting room.

"There's that funny obsessive look again," commented Dave.

"Yeah," replied Chuck. "Sure wish I knew what was going on. You don't think he's trying to sell the company, do you?"

"Nah," said Dave. "I don't know what's going on with him, but I don't think its that. Oh, well, might as well get back to work."

With that, they walked into the meeting room and got ready to go back to work.

*   *   *

"Let's take a look at the next step in our Planning Process," said Mike as he opened the next phase of the meeting. Amy, why don't you read it off of the slide up there?"

Amy complied. "Set financial goals and get a balance among **profit, cash flow,** and **equity**."

"Now" said Mike, "can anyone tell me why it's important to get a balance among these three things?"

"Because all three things are important to the financial well-being of the company" said Dave. "The company needs profits to repay its bank debt and to grow. But, if all of its profits are tied up in accounts receivable, inventory, or high debt payments, it won't have enough money to pay its bills. So that's why cash flow is important. And if we don't retain enough of our profit every year, we won't have the financial stability to weather a business downturn."

"Couldn't have said it better myself," said Mike. "Now, have you ever had goals like these before?"

The group discussed this among themselves. Like a lot of companies, they had implied goals of making enough money for a large owners salary and generous management team bonuses, with enough profit left over to pay bank debt. And at times in the company's history, they had even had goals that expressed profits as a percentage of sales. But they had never had expressed goals for all three of these elements. After several minutes of discussion it was apparent that cash flow was a definite priority. However, the group was unable to agree on specific targets and goals.

Mike finally interjected: "Well, it seems like we have another follow up item, Jerry. We've agreed that cash flow is a priority, but the company needs to set specific goals and targets."

Jerry replied, "Yep. Say, Mike, maybe we should jump to number 9 on the slides:

⑨ Identify industry trends and set product goals

"I think we need to talk about the **company's** priorities before we discuss **financial** priorities."

"That's a really good point, Jerry," replied Mike. "OK, what does Cleveland Electronics see as its major business challenges and opportunities?"

Amy interjected, "Actually, Mike, we knew that the answer to that question was going to have a lot to do with what we'd be discussing here in Marathon. So, Jerry's had us discussing these issues during the past couple of weeks. We've come up with some answers which the team had me document in this mini-business plan."

"That's great, Amy," said Mike. "Why don't you guys give **me** a presentation for the next half hour or so?"

"Glad to!" the group exclaimed.

With that, the group laid out what they saw as Cleveland Electronics' business opportunities, threats, key issues, and priorities for the next three years. Much of the discussion centered on industry trends toward manufacturing in less costly countries like China, Indonesia and Korea. In order for Cleveland Electronics to compete in the future, the company would need to become much more active in sourcing and exploiting sales opportunities in these overseas areas.

"And," said Jerry, "we're going to need to go a step beyond even that."

"You mean opening a facility in China?" asked Mike.

"Exactly," said Chuck. "We've already had one customer asking about our timeline for doing this. As more of our customers look at moving manufacturing operations to China, they are asking us if we'll be able to supply them. And you know what the answer better be if we want to keep their business."

The team discussed this issue for a while longer, and decided that, in addition to simply allowing the company to make money at its present level of sales, the issue of globalization was the other important area that needed to be addressed in the next few years. The team went over their top five customers and products, and talked about how globalization would impact their key relationships and products. They saw that adequately addressing globalization issues would require the same kind of focused continuous action over an extended period of time that addressing their other issues would require. As the discussion wound down, the team decided that their three-year goal would be focused more on **survival** than on **growth**. And, successfully surviving would take profitability levels higher than recent historical levels.

"What does that mean in terms of profits as a percentage of sales?" asked Mike.

"In the good old days, we thought of ten percent as a good strong number," replied Dave. "I'd think if we could do that again, we'd be happy."

"Happy, but not realistic," remarked Jerry.

The rest of the group agreed.

"Now," said Mike, "let's see if we can go back to Step 7—profits, cash flow and equity. Can we project sales for the next three years?" That question sparked a discussion that resulted in the following white board chart:

	Year		
	1	2	3
Sales ($ millions)	25	25	26
Profit %	5	6	8
Profits ($ millions)	1.3	1.5	2.1

"Well," said Dave, "we have profits, but a half hour ago we said that cash flow was our real priority. So now we need to work profits back to cash flow."

"Take us through it, Dave," said Mike, encouragingly.

Dave continued, "Let's first talk about the five main differences between profits and cash flow."

With that, Dave went into a ten-minute discussion of the five key differences between profit and cash flow. These differences are important because many companies manage cash flow by individually managing profits and each of these five items. Dave was able to illustrate the process using the following diagram on the white board:

    Profits

+   Depreciation

+   Working capital (increase) decrease

+   Bank borrowing increase (decrease)

+   Capital investment (increase) decrease

+   Owner investment increase (decrease)

=   Cash flow

For Cleveland Electronics, which was an S-Corporation that has no income tax liability of its own, "Profits" mean pre-tax income on the company's income statement. In calculating a cash flow number from a company's profits, the profit figure needs to be decreased for an increase in working capital such as inventory and accounts receivable. Conversely, any decrease in working capital would be added to profits in calculating cash flow,

When Dave took the group through this, the next step was to work the numbers for Cleveland Electronics:

	Year		
	1	2	3
Profits	1.3	1.5	2.1
+ Depreciation	.6	.7	.8
+ or - Working capital	0.2	0.1	-0.3
+ or - Bank debt		0.5	0.7
+ or - Capital investment		-0.7	-1
+ or - Equity investment		-0.5	-0.8
= Cash flow	2.1	1.6	1.5
Beginning cash balance	-0.7	1.4	3.0
Ending cash balance	1.4	3.0	4.5

Jerry and the management team spent a lot of time discussing and changing the above exhibit. When the discussion was about to wrap up, Jerry exclaimed,

"Well team, that four and a half million dollar cash balance at the end of Year 3 looks pretty good. I'm sure we'll have a portion of that available to share with you folks for your part in making it happen."

"Excellent point, Jerry," said Mike. "We'll definitely need another 'to do' on our list—'Develop incentive comp plan for the management team.' Now, let me make a few observations here so that we don't get confused when we get back to Cleveland."

"What you've just done here is set targets that you want Cleveland Electronics to achieve over the next three years. The way you're going to hit those targets is by developing strategies, tactics and action steps that will generate the kind of numbers you just put up on the board. These strategies, tactics and action steps will be focused and implemented because of the company's infrastructure (planning, systems and management) that we've been developing, tuning and will be implementing when we get back to Cleveland."

"In other words, Mike, you want to know if we're all clear on the differences between

> Strategies
>
> Tactics
>
> Action steps
>
> Infrastructure
>
> Systems, and
>
> Management?"

asked Amy.

"Not just the differences, Amy," replied Mike. "I want to be sure you understand how all of these interrelate and work in order to get the company to where you want it to be."

"I think we're all starting to understand," said Jerry. "But I'd like to ask one more question, if I may. Are we supposed to focus on the numbers we want to hit as we go through these strategies, tactics and action steps?"

"Let me try to answer that," said Chuck.

"Be my guest," replied Mike.

"Although the numbers we just put up on the board are our goal, just focusing on the numbers doesn't mean we're going to hit them. Like we discussed before, numbers are the **result** of what the company does—not the cause. That's why it's important to map out the company's activities and to establish accountability over them—it's the activities that will get us to the goals, not simply the goals themselves."

> "...numbers are the result of what the Company does—not the cause..."

"Excellent, Chuck!" exclaimed Mike. "Now, let's look at our Ten Point Planning Process again."

When the group did this, they lined out the steps they had completed, and their slide looked like this:

Ten Point Planning Process

1) ~~Determine mission/vision/core values/guiding principles~~

2) ~~Define the business you are in~~

3) ~~Set growth goals: Phase I, Phase II, Phase III~~

4) ~~Determine key jobs and get the right people in them. Define the management team.~~

5) ~~Determine what is needed to get harmony in the management team and/or family~~

6) ~~Define manager accountability~~

7) Set financial goals to get a balance among:

   ~~-Profit~~

   ~~-Cash flow~~

   ~~-Equity~~

8) ~~Identify core systems and determine what is needed to make them~~ work

9) ~~Identify industry trends and set product goals (stars and cash cows)~~

10) Create action plans: Assign responsibilities, budgets and target dates

"Well, folks," said Mike, "I think that's an excellent morning's work. What say we break for lunch and try to get back here by 1:30?"

With that, the meeting adjourned to the cars for lunch.

Chapter 30

Mike took the team to Seven-Mile Grill, a "Keysey" open air restaurant and bar just before the longest bridge in the Keys, descriptively named Seven-Mile Bridge. They were seated at a table adjoining the bar. Halfway through lunch, Amy, always sensitive to the sights and sounds around her, picked up a discussion between two well-dressed (for the Keys) businessmen at the bar.

"Yeah, Rich, its really a shame. He was really doing well until about a year ago. Then…I don't know…his bank account started overdrafting, vendors in town started to complain about not being paid, and the yacht club posted his name on the bulletin board for not paying his monthly bill."

"I don't know, Ed. The bank has a long relationship with Frank, but when we start to see cash flow dry up, we get concerned."

After listening in for a few more minutes, Amy picked up that Ed was an accountant and Rich the banker for a local Marathon furniture store. The store-owner, Frank, had been a bank customer for many years, but suddenly started to have trouble with liquidity.

Amy related the story to Mike. Coincidentally, Mike was familiar with the story. He had purchased several items at the store when he was furnishing his place in Marathon.

One of the well-dressed gentlemen at the bar-Ed the accountant-looked up and spotted Mike at the table with his group.

"Hey, Mike," said Ed with a wave.

"Hiyuh, Ed," replied Mike. "How's it going?"

"Not too bad, not too bad," drawled Ed slowly. "It'd be going a lot better, though, if I could talk Rich here into not pulling the plug on my good client Frank's Furniture."

"Well," said Mike, "it sounds like that's nothing a couple of Seven Mile Shooters wouldn't fix." A Seven Mile Shooter was the name of a potent blend of hard liquor followed by a glass of imported beer—a drink Mike invented when he first came down to the Keys.

"That's the first thing I tried," replied Ed. "But I think Rich here has a wooden leg. He's not going to give in."

"Too bad," said Mike with a grin. "You know, I had the idea that Frank was doing really well. Every time I went in there, he seemed to have more and more items on the floor. Even rented additional space in that T-shirt shop next to him."

"I think that's the problem," Rich (the banker) replied. "He's been showing wonderful profits on his financial statements over the past 18 months. But I think that those profits have been going straight into inventory."

"Don't you guys finance his inventory?" interjected Jerry.

"Yes, but the best we'll go is 40 % of cost," replied Rich. "And, we have the bank's total loan exposure capped at a certain level as well. Frank's been at the maximum loan amount for six months now."

"Sounds a lot like a discussion we had a little over an hour ago," exclaimed Chuck.

"Tell me about it," said Ed.

"Well," interjected Jerry quickly, "we were just talking about the relationship of profits and cash flow. Just because profits are strong doesn't mean that cash flow is good."

"Precisely," replied Ed. "In fact, with the slow down in business in the past two years, I believe that cash flow has become even more important than profits."

"I agree," said Dave.

Rich observed, "You know, we bankers are always concerned about the quality of a company's management and systems. And one of the best indicators of that quality is something called 'working capital discipline.' Without it we find many companies whose profits end up tied up in high inventory or accounts

"...and one of the best indicators of the quality of a company's management is...'working capital discipline'..."

receivable balances. In fact, I like to give my customers the old 'cork in a bottle' philosophy."

"What's that, Rich?" asked Amy.

"I like to tell them that the profits in their financial statements are like a fine wine in a bottle. But high inventory and receivables are like the cork in the bottle. The customer will never get to enjoy the wine (profits) unless they can get the cork out of the bottle by reducing inventory and receivables."

"And thereby convert profits to cash flow," added Dave.

"Yep."

"Rich, how do your customers do this?" asked Mike with a wink.

"Good systems, good management, and good planning," said Rich.

"Couldn't have said it better myself," said Jerry. "OK, crew, let's get back to work, shall we?"

With that, Jerry and company headed back to the Holiday Inn.

Chapter 31

1:30 PM. The Holiday Inn. The group is just back from lunch and is raring to go. Mike has just announced that if they work extra hard, it's possible they can finish tonight and spend tomorrow doing something outdoors. Mike brings the group's attention to the chart:

"OK, Jerry," said Mike. "Do you still have the list of open items from Phase Two of the slide show?"

With that, Jerry wrote the items on the white board:

*Accounting and finance
- -Operating budget
- -Capital budget
- -Financial data interpretation

*Systems and IT
- -Management/technical personnel selection
- -Core systems

*Sales and marketing
- -One-year sales plan

*Operations
- -Operations control
- -Finished goods inventory control

*Management and leadership
- -Build an aligned management team
- -Determine responsibilities and expectations of key jobs

*Personnel

    -Incentive sales compensation

    -Management and technical training

*Business strategy and planning

    -One to three-year business plan

    -Product or services strategy

    -Design action plans as part of business planning

"OK, and now do you have the list of follow up items you've been making note of during the past two days?" asked Mike.

Jerry wrote these on another white board:

    —Policies for hiring, firing and evaluating our employees

    —Filling VP of sales position

    —Coming up with a program for training and development of management and supervisors

    —Job descriptions, including accountabilities, for all employees, including managers

    —How to deal with China

    —Incentive/profit sharing for management team

"Now, does anyone see anything funny about these items?" asked Mike.

Chuck responded, "Yes. A few of these are duplicative."

"All right, Chuck," said Mike. "How about lining out the duplicates?"

After Chuck finished his work, the white boards looked like this:

*Accounting and finance

    -Operating budget

    -Capital budget

    -Financial data interpretation

*Systems and IT

    -Management/technical personnel selection

    -Core systems

*Sales and marketing
  -One-year sales plan

*Operations
  -Operations control
  -Finished goods inventory control

*Management and leadership
  -Build an aligned management team
  ~~-Determine responsibilities and expectations of key~~ jobs

*Personnel
  -Incentive sales compensation
  -Management and technical training

*Business strategy and planning
  -One to three-year business plan
  -Product or services strategy
  -Design action plans as part of business planning

—Policies for hiring, firing and evaluating our employees

—How to deal with China

—Incentive/profit sharing for management team

—Filling VP of sales position

~~—Coming up with a program for training and development of management and supervisors~~

—Job descriptions, including accountabilities, for all employees, including managers

Amy then said, "And it seems like three or four of the last items on the list really belong under the Personnel heading."

"OK, Amy, could you put those there?"

When Amy was finished, the group was left with one list that looked like this:

*Accounting and finance
  -Operating budget

-Capital budget

-Financial data interpretation

*Systems and IT

-Management/technical personnel selection

-Core systems

*Sales and marketing

-One-year sales plan

*Operations

-Operations control

-Finished goods inventory control

*Management and leadership

-Build an aligned management team

*Personnel

-Incentive sales compensation

-Management and technical training

-Policies for hiring, firing and evaluating our employees

-Job descriptions, including accountabilities for all employees, including management

-Filling VP of sales position

-Incentive/profit sharing for management team

*Business strategy and planning

-One to three-year business plan

-Product or services strategy

-Design action plans as part of business planning

-How to deal with China

"So, Mike, what do we have here?" asked Dave.

"Why doesn't Jerry tell us?" suggested Mike.

"Fair enough," replied Jerry.

"First of all, we need to think back to some of the work we've already done. Before we came down to Marathon, we worked on several of the first few points of the Ten Point Business Planning Process Mike gave us, remember?"

"Sure," everyone replied.

"And when we completed those items, we had our mission, vision, core values and guiding principles down, right?"

"Right," the group replied.

"And then we determined what business we were in, right?"

"Right again," everyone exclaimed.

"So!" exclaimed Jerry triumphantly, "If you take our mission, vision, core values, guiding principles, and the definition of the business we're in, the items on the white board are the remaining things we have to do to insure that everyone in the company is pulling towards the same goals, in the same way."

"Very good," said Mike, reinforcing Jerry's conclusion. "And, don't forget you already have a number of things in place that will insure this. Remember, the items on the white board are simply the things the company has **left** to do."

"Right," exclaimed Jerry, triumphantly. "Now. Where do we go from here?"

Mike replied, "It's obvious that we're not going to have time to finish the whole 'to do' list. A few of those items by themselves are in fact major projects."

"Yeah," interjected Chuck, "like a 'one to three year business plan'."

"Yes," said Dave, "and like an 'operating and capital budget'."

"And how about 'Design action plans as a part of business planning'," said Amy. "Wow, now there's a tall order!"

"As a matter of fact," said Mike, "that's the one we're going to get working on right now."

"How can we do that if we aren't even going to do the one to three year business plan until after we get back to Cleveland?" asked Chuck.

"Chuck, what do you think we've been doing the whole time we've been down here? Aren't these exercises in fact a part of business planning?" asked Dave.

After a ten-minute discussion, the team decided that in fact Dave was right.

"Now, class," said Mike, "let's get into designing action steps. And, by the way, this is the point at which we stop talking and start implementing."

"So, a new phase in Cleveland Electronics' development?" asked Jerry.

"Right you are," replied Mike. "Now, let me introduce you to one of the most powerful little pieces of paper I've ever come across." With that, Mike passed out a paper like this to each team member:

Key Issue	Discussion	Action Steps	Responsible Person	Due Date	✔ = Complete

"What's so powerful about this blank form?" asked Jerry.

"Jerry, it gets its power from you and the team. Be patient awhile and I'll explain."

"Sorry, chief," said Jerry. "Its just that I'm getting a little excited now that we're getting closer to the answers."

"No problem, Jerry," replied Mike. "Now, the first step in the whole process is easy. See all of those 'to do's' on that white board? Head up each piece of paper with one of those 'to dos'.

When the team was done, they had further combined and narrowed their list of seventeen items down to nine key issues.

"Now," said Mike, "let's put these little doggies in order by priority. In other words, the most important item will go on top of the stack. The least important on the bottom of the stack."

This last instruction sparked a lively discussion. After about a half-hour, the team had ordered the pieces of paper as follows:

#1 **Build an aligned management team**

#2 **Operations control**

#3 **Systems and IT**

    -Management/technical personnel selection

    -Core systems

    -Finished goods inventory control

#4 **Business strategy and planning**

    -One to three-year business plan

    -Product or services strategy

#5 **Accounting and finance**

    -Operating budget

    -Capital budget

    -Financial data interpretation

#6 **Sales and marketing**

    -One-year sales plan

    -Filling VP of sales position

#7 **Job descriptions, including accountabilities for all employees, including management**

#8 **Policies for hiring, firing, and evaluating our employees**

#9 **Management and technical training**

#10 **Incentive/profit sharing plan for management team**

#11 **How to deal with China**

"OK, genius, now what?" asked Jerry.

"Now, we are going to talk about how these little pieces of paper are going to help you change your company," replied Mike. "First of all, we call this stack of forms the start of an **Issue/Action Agenda**. The reason we call it that is that its function is to map key action steps to key issues the company is trying to resolve."

"In other words," said Chuck, "it develops FOCUS."

"Right," replied Mike. "And it does another important thing—it establishes accountability for completing action steps on a timely basis."

"I'm starting to see the light, here, Mike, but it's a dim one."

"Stop interrupting Jerry, and hopefully the light will come up a little," replied Mike, a little testily this time. "Let's talk about how we're going to use these things. In fact, let's play 'pretend.' It's now two weeks from today, and you folks are holding your first implementation meeting."

"Implementation meeting?" asked Amy.

"OOPS, Amy, you're right again," said Mike. "I screwed up. I haven't explained about those yet, have I?"

"Nice to hear a little humility coming from the consultant," snickered Jerry.

"Well, anyway," continued Mike, "when you get back to Cleveland, we're going to set up implementation meetings. Right now, I'd recommend two hours, every two weeks."

"Just what we need," quipped Jerry, "more meetings."

"Yes Jerry," replied Mike, "but because of how we are going to structure them, these will be among the most productive and profitable meetings your company has ever had. Anyway, at first I'll moderate these meetings. The stack of forms you have in front of you is the agenda for the meeting. As you discuss each key issue, the moderator takes notes on discussion, action steps, due dates, etc. The aim is to get four or five action steps down for each key item. With me so far?"

Nodding heads told Mike they were.

"Now," continued Mike, "one rule of the meetings is that before you leave one issue for the next one, the group must have decided on action steps—in other words, WHO will do WHAT by WHEN. Only when these questions are answered to the group's satisfaction can the discussion proceed to the next issue. Still with me?"

Again, all heads nodded.

"Now," said Mike, "a few more rules."

"Hey Mike, I'm getting a little sick of all of these rules," remarked Jerry. "You know, I never liked rules when I was a kid, and I don't much like them now—except when they're for other people," Jerry finished with a chuckle.

"OK, Jerry. Let's just call them suggestions then, all right?"

"That sounds kind of wishy-washy," said Chuck.

"Chuck, remember, in the real world, there is no such thing as a 'sure thing.' Therefore, 'suggestions' is actually a better term than "rules." I like to compare these 'suggestions' to insurance. Because in the real world there is no such thing as a sure thing, these suggestions are like dollars you pay on an insurance policy. The more of them you do, the more likely it is that you'll get the desired result. But no one can guarantee you the result—unless they're living in fantasyland."

> "...in the real world there is no such thing as a sure thing, these suggestions are like dollars you pay on an insurance policy. The more of them you do, the more likely it is that you'll get the desired result..."

"I've never heard a consultant say that before," remarked Jerry.

"So, Jerry, let's not hear about my lack of humility any more," retorted Mike.

The group laughed.

"OK, now back to these 'suggestions'. I SUGGEST that the attitude you all take within the meeting room is that each of you are consultants trying to work together to solve the company's issues. No one of you is smart enough to be able to solve these issues all by yourselves. All of you together need to bring your experience and strength to bear on these issues. However, once the meeting is over, the person responsible for the action step calls the shots. Understood?"

"Sort of like follow the chain of command?" asked Dave.

"Sort of but not exactly," said Mike. "But following the chain of command along the lines of the company's new organization chart is another ru—uh—sorry, suggestion."

"Any more suggestions?" asked Jerry, impatiently.

> "But following the chain of command along the lines of the company's new organization chart is another…suggestion."

"Yes. Another suggestion is that the meeting ends when the two hours are up."

"Even if we're not completely through all of our issues?" asked Dave.

"Yep," replied Mike. "Remember, you all still have to run the company on top of building all of this infrastructure. And one two-hour meeting will result in plenty of action steps. Remember that you're going to prioritize your issues at the beginning of each meeting. Therefore, by limiting the time spent at each meeting, you'll automatically be focusing your energies on the company's most important issues. Working this way insures that the more important issues get resolved first."

"Any more suggestions, Mike?"

"There will be more suggestions," replied Mike, "but we'll make them up along the way. For now, why don't we get right into our two-hour meeting? It's now 2:30. Let's go until 4:30, then we'll see where we are."

Following the suggestions just outlined, Mike led the team through their first implementation meeting. At first, the group had trouble staying focused on the issue on the table. Some of the issues were related to one another, so discussion tended to jump from one issue to another. Mike was able to keep the team on focus, however, by always returning to the primary issue on the table, and not allowing the group to move on until they had formulated initial action steps for each issue.

Around 4:30, Mike said, "OK, group. Let's take a breather and see where we are." Amy, as the note taker for the meeting, had completed the first two issues as follows:

Key Issue	Discussion	Action Steps	Responsible Person	Due Date	✔ = Complete
1. Build an aligned management team.	We need a new format for managing the company. Everyone reporting to Jerry using our old "rake" management structure no longer works.	1. Discuss the organization chart developed yesterday with other managers at the company. Confirm their roles and responsibilities.	Jerry	06//15/03	
	We need a "stacked" organization chart, and management needs to follow the chain of command.	2. Publish the new org chart and hold a company meeting of all employees to explain the new organization and answer questions.	Amy	06/30/03	
	Managers need to have clearly defined goals, objectives and responsibilities and be held accountable for them.	3. Develop job descriptions and accountabilities for each member of the senior management team: Jerry Amy Chuck Dave V.P. Sales	Jerry Amy Chuck Dave Jerry	05/31/03 05/31/03 05/31/03 05/31/03 06/30/03	
		4. Meet with each member of the senior management team to review and approve their job descriptions, goals and accountabilities: Jerry Amy Chuck Dave VP of Sales	Jerry Jerry Jerry Jerry Jerry	06/30/03 07/15/03 07/31/03 07/15/03 08/15/03	
		5. Hire new VP of sales	Jerry	07/31/03	

Key Issue	Discussion	Action Steps	Responsible Person	Due Date	✔ = Complete
1. Build an aligned management team (continued).	The senior management team needs to fill gaps in their knowledge of general management and leadership techniques.	6. Contact Cleveland area manufacturers association to determine availability of management training course.	Amy	06/15/03	
		7. Meet with each senior management team member and determine the management training courses they should be taking in the next 12 months	Amy	08/15/03	
		8. Emphasize company goals, objectives, core values, guiding principles at management team and company meetings.	Jerry	Ongoing	
2. Operations control	Chuck may not have the proper people reporting to him. Many people in production were promoted based on their technical proficiency rather than how well they could manage people and workflow.	1. Perform a strengths/weaknesses inventory of each key supervisor— supervisors, team leaders, head of engineering, production foreman, shift supervisors.	Chuck	07/01/03	
		2. Discuss each key supervisor with Jerry and decide whether to retain, train or terminate the individual.	Chuck	07/31/03	

Key Issue	Discussion	Action Steps	Responsible Person	Due Date	✔ = Complete
2. Operations control (continued)	The existing job tracking system is not working well. Job status and backlog figures across all departments are inadequate or non-existent.	3. Review report of prior consultant regarding this system. Develop action steps to implement those recommendations deemed appropriate.	Chuck	08/31/03	
		4. If necessary, develop cross-functional team comprised of reps from production, engineering, quality assurance, and scheduling. Purpose of team would be to further investigate and make additional recommendations concerning the job tracking system.	Dave	09/30/03	
	The procedures for inputting changes to the job tracking system are vague and not well know. Written procedural documentation was not revised when the new system was installed 2 years ago.	5. After steps 3 and 4, above are complete, need to decide whether a team should be appointed to re-document the system.	Dave	10/15/03	
	Our rework percentages have exceeded 2 % for 5 of the last 7 months. This is not acceptable.	6. Review and discuss existing scrap and rework reports with department heads. Determine that necessary corrective action has been taken. See pages 15-22 of prior consultant report for recommendations	Chuck	09/15/03	

"Well team," said Mike, "do you think you have a feel for how these meetings are supposed to go?

"I think so, Mike," answered Chuck. "But the whole idea of this is, these action steps have to be completed, right?"

"You're right on," replied Mike. "But remember, by using these meetings and the Issue/Action agenda, you're enforcing accountability as well as deciding appropriate action steps. It's the accountability that insures that these actions will be completed."

"OK, Mike," said Jerry. "How about we break up now and meet again right here at 8:00 AM tomorrow?"

"Jerry, Mike said he thought we could take the day off tomorrow and maybe go fishing or lay on the beach," reminded Amy.

"Yeah, Amy, but I feel like we've got a head of steam running here, and I'd like to keep pushing on," said Chuck.

"Yeah, me too," replied Dave. "We've got a long way to go before the company's turned around, and I'd just as soon keep working on the company as long as we have the time."

"I'm with you, Dave," replied Jerry. "Mike, what do you say?"

"Gees, folks," replied Mike, "I was hoping to take you all out to a great little grouper spot I know…"

"We can do that some other time, Mike. Right now, we're all focused, so let's just keep on working," replied Jerry.

"Here's a suggestion," said Mike. "Why don't we bring dinner in here and work until around ten or eleven tonight. That way, we can probably get through a few more issues, and we can still go fishing in the morning."

Jerry's thoughts immediately turned to the silver Cobb. *"And there goes my chance to get Gina the best birthday present ever,"* his brain whined.

Jerry then exclaimed, "Why, Mike, I'm surprised at you. You're suggesting we break one of your rules. 'Implementation meetings will last no longer than two hours.' Didn't we just hear that a couple of hours ago?"

"Uh….yes," said Mike, "I did say that."

"And, Mike, I think that's a good rule," said Amy. "We're all pretty tired right now. And the last two hours have been pretty *in-tense*. I think we all need to relax, maybe do our own thing tonight, and then hit it again in the morning."

"OK," said Mike, "But if we invoke the two hour rule again…"

"Right," said Jerry. "Maybe we'll still be able to get some recreation in before we catch the plane tomorrow."

With that, the group finalized plans to meet first thing in the morning. Mike gave them various suggestions for entertainment and dinner, then said good night.

Jerry said that he had an old friend he was going to try to see that evening, so Amy, Dave and Chuck were on their own for dinner. The meeting adjourned.

Chapter 32

A few minutes later. Jerry tried three times more to call Amber. No response other than the answering machine. With his heart beating a little faster than normal, he picked up the yellow pages…

"…Hmmm…Herbie's…Overseas Highway. If I remember right, that's over the other side of the airport. I'll just grab a quick dinner from room service, shower and shave, and head over there. Hopefully Amber's working tonight, and she still has the coin."

An hour or so later, Jerry was heading over the Vaca Cut bridge on the way to Herbie's. The sun was setting, and the view to Jerry's right was 'way beyond beautiful. The soft blues, pinks and purples of a glorious Keys sunset is enough to make an observer want to never go home. Sights like this make for many fervent wishes that Keys sunsets last forever.

"This is too beautiful to be real," murmured Jerry to himself as the last of the sun dipped below the horizon.

He shivered with the anticipation of once again seeing Amber. Once he passed the Marathon airport, he paid close attention to the businesses and addresses on the left-hand side of US Highway 1, the main road through the Keys. Finally, he began to recognize some of the buildings and signs from his first trip down to see Mike—when he first met Amber. But, when he finally saw the sign that said "Herbie's," Jerry's heart almost stopped. For right under that sign was another sign-a smaller sign. It read, "CLOSED."

Jerry couldn't believe it. He pulled up in front of the place. Sure enough, there was no sign of life. Doors were locked, windows were soaped out, and the parking lot was barren.

After sitting a few minutes, he thought, *"Well, maybe I can drive down to Key West tomorrow and pick up a coin and have it made into jewelry. Mike said something about Mel Fisher's estate having a store down there. But, jeez, that coin of Amber's sure would have been perfect..."*

With that, Jerry started driving. He continued going west on US Highway 1, towards the town of Key West, an hour's drive away. For a few minutes, he thought about heading there tonight. But he eventually found himself driving over the Seven-Mile Bridge and the dramatic beauty of the Atlantic Ocean on his left and the Gulf on his right soon took his mind over. The magic of sunset, even in the rapidly fading light, which turned the sky and waters various shade of gray, was still too much to ignore. After crossing the bridge, Jerry turned the car around and headed back toward Marathon, the majestic water views capturing his attention for yet another Seven-Mile Bridge crossing.

As the car came back into Marathon, Jerry noticed a white banner under Dick & Odette's main restaurant sign. "Live entertainment nightly," proclaimed the sign.

"Just the ticket. I'll pull in, listen to a decent band for an hour, then call it a night, go back to the hotel and call Gina."

Jerry entered the restaurant. Just before entering the bar area was another sign announcing the entertainment for the evening:

Now appearing

In our lounge

First time in the Keys...

Amber and the LO-LO's!!!

"Huh," thought Jerry. *"What a coincidence. That can't be the same Amber I've been looking for these past few days. Wonder what the 'Lo-Los' are?"*

He sat down at a table where he'd have a good view of the stage. When the waitress took Jerry's drink order, he asked, "What kind of a band do you have playing tonight?"

The waitress replied, "Oh, it's not a band, it's a comedy act."

"A comedy act!" exclaimed Jerry. "Just what I need. When do they get started?"

"What time is it?" asked the waitress.

"Oh, just about nine o'clock," replied Jerry.

"Then they'll be getting started any minute now," replied the waitress.

Jerry sat back with his drink. Dick the bar owner stepped up on stage to introduce the act.

"Ladies and gentlemen, welcome to Dick and Odette's. Tonight, we're very proud to present one of the funniest comedy teams I've ever had the pleasure of viewing. Introducing.... *Amber...and...her...LO-LOs*!!!"

With that, a small, thin, very tan woman entered the stage from a side entrance hidden by a curtain. Accompanying her on a wheeled cart were two live parrots. The birds were sitting on their perches, and were already starting to talk to one another in loud parrot-speak.

Jerry's jaw dropped. His mouth was hanging wide open because...incredible as it seemed...**this** Amber was **his** Amber! Or, at least, the Amber he'd been trying to get hold of for the past few days. *"Incredible,"* Jerry thought. *"Unbelievable,"* his mind exclaimed again a few seconds later.

After opening with a few very funny jokes poking fun at a couple of the locals in the Keys, "conchs," as they're called, Amber introduced her feathered friends.

"I suppose you're all wondering why I call them the Lo-Lo's?"

A couple of voices from the bar confirmed her question.

"Well," said Amber, "just listen."

With that, Amber began singing a song to the tune of "Battle Hymn of the Republic:

Lo-lo-lo-lo-lo-lo-lo-lo-lo-lo-lo..."

Before she was two bars into the song, the parrots immediately joined in:

"Lo-lo-lo-lo-lo-lo-lo-lo-lo-lo-lo..."

Musical Lo-Los! Amber stopped her singing, and the birds continued on, through the first stanza...and the second...and all of the way through the third and final one! Even more remarkable was that the birds sang with perfect pitch, even holding notes and harmonizing with one another as they went through the song.

When the birds' performance ended, the audience erupted with much applause, and even gave the birds a standing ovation. Amber, beaming, thanked the crowd profusely, and then told some funny stories and jokes about living in the Keys.

After about 45 minutes, the act drew to a close.

"And don't forget to come see me on the weekend," Amber reminded her audience. "On Friday and Saturday nights, I do two shows at eight and ten. Tell your friends!"

With that, Amber and the Lo-Lo's left the stage to another round of applause.

A few minutes later, Amber went up to the bar and ordered a beer. Jerry immediately rose from his table, went over to the bar, and lightly touched Amber on the shoulder.

"Hi," began Jerry. "Remember me?"

"Jerry! How are you!" exclaimed Amber with a smile.

"I've been just great, kiddo, but I'll be even better if you tell me you've still got that Cobb."

"Of course," replied Amber. "But now I'm not so sure I want to sell it. This comedy act's pretty lucrative, with what Dick's paying me and the tips and all."

With that, Amber bent over, and emptied the tip bucket at the edge of the small stage.

"Wow!" exclaimed Jerry. "Looks like about $45 or $50 in there."

"Yep," Amber said proudly. "And it's even better on the weekends."

Jerry went on to describe how he had been trying to get in touch with her, and his surprise at finding her doing a comedy act at Dick and Odette's. Amber got a little bit friendlier, even seeming to encourage Jerry's asking a few more questions.

Jerry then asked, "Well, Amber, how did you ever manage to switch from waitressing to comedy?"

"A very good question," replied Amber.

"It all started in college. One of my childhood friends went to Northwestern. I was a student at Loyola."

"So you were originally from Chicago?" asked Jerry.

"Right," replied Amber. "Northwestern has an excellent acting school, and it just so happened that my friend's roommate was Shelly Long."

Jerry interrupted, "You mean *the* Shelly Long?"

"Yep," answered Amber. "Only at that time, she was only a student, struggling just like the rest of us. Anyway, we hung around together, and Shelly started to encourage me to develop my sense of humor. She even suggested that I get acquainted with Second City, which at that time had a school for students of improvisation."

"And did you enjoy comedy at the time?" asked Jerry.

"Oh, yes, very much so," replied Amber. "But at the time, I wanted to be a teacher, also, so eventually the pressures of getting through Loyola, getting certified, and starting the teaching career left zero energy left for comedy. Then, about five years ago, my marriage broke up, and I moved down to the Keys. I had gotten tired of teaching, so I just kept picking up waitress jobs in between learning to scuba dive and looking for sunken treasure."

"Did you like it?" asked Jerry, who, by this time, was fascinated.

"I liked the money," replied Amber. "But I somehow always felt that when it came to performing, I really belonged back in comedy."

"Then why didn't you just get back into comedy?" asked Jerry.

"Well," replied Amber, "you see, it's not that easy. It takes a while to get back into writing your own material, then you have to practice, then I had to try and find something unique…"

"Like the parrots," said Jerry.

"Yes, like the parrots," said Amber. "It takes a lot of time, and it's not as easy as it sounds. I just could never get focused enough to really get going on comedy again, until…"

"Until?" replied Jerry.

"Yes, until I met this guy in a bar one night. He was some kind of business consultant. I was telling him how I'd really like to get into comedy again, but I couldn't seem to focus on doing the things it would take to get there. He suggested that I use this thing that he had his business clients use. He said it would help me develop the kind of continuous, focused action over an extended period of time that I'd need to get my act together—no pun intended."

"Uh, oh," said Jerry.

"What?" replied Amber.

"This guy's name wouldn't be Mike, would it?"

"Why, yes. Mike Henderson. He comes in here once in a while. Do you know him?"

Jerry just laughed. He then related the story of how he had met Mike and began coming down to the Keys. He and Amber had a few good laughs at the coincidence of it all, and an hour passed all too quickly.

"So, Jerry, are the things that Mike's telling you what you need to know in order to fix your company?"

"They seem to be, although the real proof will come when we get back to Cleveland and start putting them into practice. I guess I've seen from the results you and a couple of other people down here have gotten that what Mike's telling me really does work."

"It works if you work it," responded Amber.

"Yeah. That's a good one," said Jerry. "I'll have to remember to tell the team that tomorrow. And speaking about business, let's talk about your Cobb again. After you showed it to me at Herbies, it seems like I've been thinking about it every day. About how great it'd look hanging around my wife Gina's neck…"

"OK, OK, Jerry," interrupted Amber with a smile. "I see where this is going. If you've got your checkbook…" And right there, Amber produced the 1733 silver Cobb, put it in Jerry's hand, and closed his fingers over it.

"I hope Gina adores it," Amber said with a sigh.

Chapter 33

8:00 AM the next morning. The Holiday Inn conference room. All present and accounted for.

"OK, team, are we ready to hit it?" Mike opened the meeting.

"Yeah, let's go, we want to get out of here and enjoy some recreation before getting on the plane," said Chuck.

"Have you decided what you want to do?" asked Jerry.

"Of course. What do you think we talked about at dinner last night?" replied Dave. "It looks like Chuck and I are going to rent **Sea•Doo's** and do an eco-tour of the back country."

"The back country? What's that?" asked Jerry.

"That's the bay side of the Keys, replied Mike. There are a lot of shallows and mangrove islands in the back country. All of that creates cover and habitat for fish of all sizes—from small baitfish to huge 150-pound tarpon."

"And some sharks that get even bigger than that," said Dave.

"Oh, OK," said Jerry. "I get it now. That's where the excitement comes from, right? Riding around 150-pound sharks on a little bitty jet boat?"

"No, the excitement comes from when you fall in the water and have to get away from those toothy critters," remarked Mike.

"Are you sure the **Eco**-tour shouldn't be called the **Mako**-tour?" asked Jerry.

The team laughed. While Dave and Chuck were going on tour, Amy and Mike had decided that they would do a charter trip on one of Bob's boats, the Lucky Dog. Jerry decided to join them. "Sounds like a whole heck of a lot more fun than falling off of a jet boat and being eaten alive by sharks," Jerry said.

"Actually Jerry, there probably won't be any sharks around," replied Mike. "Sharks tend to frequent the shallows mainly at night, and very few sharks over two feet long are spotted in the back country during the day."

"Can you guaranteed that?" asked Jerry.

"No." replied Mike. "Just like with turning around companies, there are no guarantees with sharks. And no, Jerry, I wouldn't like to speculate on the difference between a shark and a turnaround consultant."

"The consultant has a more ferocious bite?" smirked Jerry.

"Yeah, you'll find out about that when you get my bill," said Mike to the laughter of the rest of the team members. "Now, let's get to work. What's the first thing we do at the beginning of each meeting?"

"We re-prioritize our issues," replied Amy.

"Right," said Mike. With that, each team member took out his or her prioritized *Issue/Action Agendas*:

#1 **Build an aligned management team**

#2 **Operations control**

#3 **Systems and IT**

-Management/technical personnel selection

-Core systems

-Finished goods inventory control

#4 **Business strategy and planning**

-One to three year business plan

-Product or services strategy

#5 **Accounting and finance**

-Operating budget

-Capital budget

-Financial data interpretation

#6 **Sales and marketing**

-One year sales plan

-Filling VP of sales position

#7 Job descriptions, including accountabilities for all employees, including management

#8 Policies for hiring, firing, and evaluating our employees

#9 Management and technical training

#10 Incentive/profit sharing for management team

#11 How to deal with China

and spent the next couple of minutes discussing the priorities. They agreed that the issues were, for now at least, to remain in their original order.

"OK, folks," said Mike. "Now, what about 'Systems and IT'?"

Jerry and the team recapped where the company had been with regard to this issue. It seems that a couple of years ago, the decision had been made to install a new IT system. The company opted to go with one of the latest "small company" ERP packages on the market at the time. Instead of delivering all of the benefits the software people promised however, it seemed like the new system never really got off of the ground. And it wasn't for lack of trying. In fact, Cleveland Electronics had gone through two heads of IT in trying to get the system fully operational. At present, the IT manager position was unfilled, and the system was functioning at a level that barely allowed the company to perform its basic functions—invoicing and collecting from customers, paying bills, doing payroll, and producing monthly financial statements.

The more the team discussed the computer system and its problems, the more it seemed like the IT system itself was the root of all of their difficulties.

Jerry remarked, "Hey, guys, I think we've finally found it! The root of all of our problems! It's that damn computer system. Why don't we re-prioritize our issues, make that the # 1 issue, and focus on getting the right system in and implemented? That might be all we need to do to get the company back on track!"

Jerry's idea fired the discussion for the next several minutes. Then Dave remarked, "Hold on. Hold on. Its seems like we've been here before."

After a few more minutes of discussion, the rest of the team agreed. Each team member could recall at least once in the last six months where a discussion among management or between management and employees had ended up blaming the majority of the company's problems on the computer system. In fact, on one such occasion, the company had called in a computer consultant to help them analyze the situation. The consultant had recommended a new feasibility study, with the eventual goal of changing to another system that better fit the company's needs.

"OK, we've used up enough time," interjected Mike suddenly. "Does anyone want to hear my impression?"

"We're going to hear it whether we want to or not," grumbled Jerry, "so go ahead."

"When I was going through the company back in Cleveland," began Mike, "I had the opportunity to interview your people. I got the impression that a lot of supervisors and employees wanted to blame the computer system for many of the problems the company has been experiencing. I was able to locate and talk to both of your former IT managers, including James, who you will recall was in charge of the original feasibility study and evaluation that resulted in the system you now have."

"To cut to the chase, Mike, what do you think?" asked Chuck.

"Well, my impression is that the system you have is fine for right now and probably the next five years. Of course, it's hard to draw that conclusion without knowing your five-year plan, which you haven't developed yet, but assuming realistic growth rates the system you have now should fit for the foreseeable future. Another observation I have is that, in a technical sense, the system was well implemented. Meaning, the software and hardware is well matched and available choices among various configuration alternatives were well made."

"If everything is so great, Mike, then why don't we have accurate information, and why does the accurate information we do have take so long to get?" asked Dave.

"Yeah, and why can't the system do a lot of things like order scheduling, job tracking, inventory control, and materials requirements planning that our man James and the software sales rep told us it could do?" asked Jerry. "Why, I think I even remember that the computer people promised us a six month pay back due to all of the money we were going to make just because of better job management."

"The main reason for those problems," said Mike, "is that, although the system is the right system and it was technically well implemented, the company never changed the way its people handled certain functions to match the way the new system is set up to handle them. So, even though your system is set up to handle 'best practices' for your industry and various applications like scheduling, inventory control, material requisitioning, etc., you folks never changed the **old** way you

> "...although the system is the right system and it was technically well implemented, the company never changed the way its people handled certain functions to match the way the new system is set up to handle them."

did business to these '**best practices**'. Until you do this, you won't get the benefits of the system that the sales rep promised."

"Isn't that like putting the cart before the horse?" asked Dave. "The way I learned it, you're supposed to pick the system that best supports the way the company does business. It sounds like you're saying it should be the other way around."

"Yes, that's exactly what I'm saying," replied Mike. "In the early days of computers, what you're saying was absolutely correct. When all you had to do was implement a simple accounting system or an inventory management system, the best thinking at the time was that you should select the package that best supported the way the company did business. However, over time, as you all know, computer systems have become more sophisticated."

> "Most large corporations handle business processes in standard fashion, because their managers are taught similar approaches in the business schools. Small companies, on the other hand, do things the way their owners set them up to do things."

"Today, most systems, like yours, do far more than just routine bookkeeping and accounting functions. Now think about how small companies do things. Most large corporations handle business processes in standard fashion, because their managers are taught similar approaches in the business schools. Small companies, on the other hand, do things the way their owners set them up to do things. These methods are only very slowly changed over time. In other words, large companies tend to have standardized approaches that make it much easier to fit an IT system to than a small company."

"I know what you mean," replied Dave. "I took a couple of IT refresher courses a couple of years back, and the professors were saying the same thing. Because small companies do things in different ways, it is much harder to try to 'fit' an IT application to a small company. So, what do we do?"

Mike continued, "Remember, we discussed that today's modern IT systems, yours included, have 'best practices' built right into them? Well, one of the steps in your action plan should be to look at the way you're doing things today, and decide whether your systems' 'best practices' may not in fact be a better way of doing these things. In those situations where you decide to switch to 'best practices', you will then need to revise and document the new best practice, and train your people in how to apply the new practice. Then, you'll need to work out the inevitable small problems that are going to occur whenever you change or start new procedures."

"Sounds like a big undertaking," remarked Amy.

"Yes, but I think Mike has something," said Jerry. "We were going to have to change and document a lot of our practices anyway. So, the really good news here is that our IT system will support a new and better way of doing business. By looking at our IT this way, I **can** see that the system is actually going to improve the company, isn't that right, Mike?"

> "So, the really good news here is that our system will support a new and better way of doing business.

"Absolutely." Mike replied. "That was great insight, Jerry."

"Now, how about the people in our IT department?" asked Chuck. "Should we be changing anything there?"

"Well, for sure, we need to get a new head of IT," replied Dave.

"How about the three people in the department right now?" asked Jerry. "Do any of them have the potential to manage the department?"

The group discussed this idea for several minutes. They concluded that, in fact, one of the people in the department could become a choice for the next IT manager. "But," interjected Dave, "I wouldn't want to say for sure right now that Brian's our man."

After more discussion, the team decided that Dave should discuss this with Brian, take a closer look at his background, training, certifications, and experience, and then decide whether to make a promotion from within.

Suddenly, Amy interjected. "Hey. Wait a minute. Shouldn't I be writing all of this down somewhere?"

"You bet," replied Mike. "On the good old **Issue/Action Agenda**. You did bring along the one from yesterday, didn't you?"

"Sure," said Amy. "I even got the chance to type it up last night when we got home from dinner."

"Good," replied Mike. "Now, let's just take the minutes of this morning's discussion following the Issue/Action Agenda format: Key Issue, Discussion, and **who** will do **what** by **when**."

After they had completed this step, the group had a couple of agenda sheets that looked like this:

Key Issue	Discussion	Action Steps	Responsible Person	Due Date	✔ = Complete
3. Systems and IT	We need to compare the way we do business to the "best practices" built into our IT system, and decide where we should change our practices	1. Select one person each from IT, production, accounting and sales to serve on a cross-functional team.	Dave	July 1	
	to those supported by the system.	2. Evaluate existing practices versus best practices embedded into the IT system and select best alternatives.	Dave	September 1	
		3. Document selected practices and develop training programs to retrain our people in selected procedures and policies.	Amy	October 15	

Key Issue	Discussion	Action Steps	Responsible Person	Due Date	✔ = Complete
3. Systems and IT (continued)		4. Evaluate IT system in 12 months to decide whether it should be changed or supplemented for increased efficiency.	Dave	June 30, 2004	
	We need to select a new IT manager. Brian may be the logical choice.	5. Develop job criteria	Dave	June 15	
		6. Interview Brian with regard to background, experience, education, certifications and career goals	Dave Jerry	July 1 July 8	
		7. Decide whether to appoint Brian IT manager on a trial basis.	Dave	August 1	
		8. If it is decided not to hire Brian as head of IT, place help wanted ads and post job on Internet.	Amy	August 5	

Dave said, "This just about covers our issues under IT, but I wonder if it adequately addresses the concerns we had about inventory control systems."

"I was just thinking the same thing," replied Chuck. "I don't know if just reviewing our policies and procedures and comparing them to 'best practices' is going to be enough."

"All right," replied Mike. "Let's talk about our concerns here."

Dave began the discussion. "It seems like our problems all started several years ago, when our customers began implementing what they call 'just in time' inventory management techniques. Over the years, we've had a few different kinds of systems—'kan-ban,' 'pull,' just to name a few. But the bottom line now is, our customers, and particularly our three largest ones, want us to mange their inventories for them. Being a small company, we can't afford the sophisticated inventory management these large companies once had. So, we end up keeping a lot of inventory on hand just so we won't run out if the customer calls."

"What are your turns down to?" asked Mike.

"We're down to about two point four five a year on the finished goods," replied Dave. "And heading lower."

"And that's no good," interjected Chuck.

"You're right," replied Mike. "I'm sure this was one of the reasons you went to the new IT system a couple of years ago, right?"

"Right," said Dave. "But once again, control over our finished goods was another benefit that has never materialized. The new system was supposed to decrease our inventory investment, decrease warehousing and handing costs, decrease our interest costs on the inventory we were carrying, and decrease the number of 'stock outs' when a customer created a demand for parts. The only thing that happened was that our 'stock outs' became non-existent. But that is only because we increased the finished goods inventory for 'cushion' against the system not working."

"And therefore," finished Mike, "your cash flow went the same way as Frank's Furniture?'

"Right!" exclaimed Jerry, remembering the discussion that they had had at lunch yesterday over at the Seven-Mile Grill.

The group discussed this issue at length. Finally, Mike remarked, "Does anyone remember their ABC's?"

"What?" Amy asked. "You mean, like in first grade?

"Nah, he probably means something having to do with the Keys," said Chuck. "Like Maybe ABC stands for 'Always Be Catching'?"

"Chuck, the phrase is 'Always Be Closing,' and we haven't talked about sales at the company yet," said Jerry.

"No, folks, I actually mean ABC as it relates to what we're talking about here. Let me talk a little about ABC inventory management, and Activity Based Costing.

"Excuse me, Mike, was that Casting?" smirked Chuck.

"No, Chuck, Costing," replied Mike. "First, ABC inventory management is a simple concept whereby you separate all of your inventory items into three categories. Category A items are critical, usually high value items that you absolutely must have in stock. Category C items are non-critical, usually low value items. Category B items are those in between Category A and C. The idea is that you use different inventory management techniques on each class of items. For example, your Category A items will be tracked on a real time basis in the computer, and you might physically count those items once a week. Your Category C items might be in the computer at their last reorder quantity, and are counted once a year. Does this make sense?"

Everyone nodded.

Mike continued. "Now, on to Activity Based Costing. This is a non-traditional way of looking at your costs, and we don't have time to go into great detail here."

"Mike," Dave interjected, "I went to several seminars on Activity Based Cost analysis five or six years ago, and we've talked about it among ourselves."

"Yep, even I am a little familiar with the concept," said Jerry.

"OK, great," said Mike. "Then I hope you all remember that one of the things companies learned when they went to Activity Based Costing was that the cost of being out-of-stock on an item far exceeded anyone's wildest imaginations."

"Yes," said Dave. "And the other thing I remember is that the cost of producing finished goods under an Activity Based Costing system varied greatly in a lot of cases from the old 'full absorption costing' model."

"Right," said Mike.

The group discussed this some more, and finally Mike reminded them that they needed to record this on the Issue/Action Agenda. When Amy was done transcribing, the Agenda looked like this:

Key Issue	Discussion	Action Steps	Responsible Person	Due Date	✔ = Complete
3. Systems and IT (continued)	Our finished goods inventory is out of control. This area will need more help that just switching to the best practices imbedded in our computer system.	9. Using Activity Based Costing, determine the cost of maintaining current inventory levels.	Dave	July 31	
		10. Perform an ABC inventory analysis on the finished good inventory.	Chuck	August 15	
		11. Review the original feasibility study and proposal for the new IT system to see how much benefit was projected from finished goods inventory reduction	Dave	August 15	
		12. Using above information and results of the "best practices" comparison, decide upon appropriate solutions to our inventory issues.	Jerry	September 1	

"Does anyone have any questions or comments before we wrap it up this morning?" asked Mike.

With that, the group engaged in five or ten minutes of discussion on the things they had learned, and expressed their eagerness to get back to Cleveland and start implementing their action plans.

"Jerry, do you think you'll be able to lead the next implementation meeting without me?" asked Mike.

"Sure," Jerry said. "But can I give you a call before the meeting and go over the rules with you one more time?"

"Absolutely," said Mike. "In fact, why don't we set the date and time of the next meeting and the date and time of that phone call right now?"

The group then set the next meeting about two weeks down the road, and Mike and Jerry worked out the time of their conference call. After these details were taken care of, Mike and Jerry wrapped up the meeting, and individual team members took off to enjoy the various activities they had planned for the rest of the day.

*   *   *

Almost two weeks later. Jerry and Mike were on the telephone discussing the implementation meeting Jerry would be leading in a couple of days.

"All right, Jerry," said Mike. "Did you have Amy type up and distribute the minutes of the meeting we had down in Marathon?"

"She said she'd have those tomorrow," replied Jerry.

"Uh, oh, replied Mike.

"What?"

"Jerry, I guess 1 forgot to tell you this little point. It always works best if you distribute the Issue/Action Agenda for the next meeting about a week before the meeting date."

> "It always works best if you distribute the Issue/Action Agenda for the next meeting about a week before the meeting date."

"Why's that?"

"Because the first thing your team members are going to do when they get it is look and see if they have any action items coming up by the date of your meeting. If you distribute the Agenda a week ahead of time, they'll have time to complete those action steps by the date of the meeting."

"Smart," remarked Jerry.

"And one other thought," said Mike. "When leading the meeting, have a six-month calendar with you, and try to set the action steps so they're due right around the time you expect to hold your implementation meetings. That way, you'll get the most benefit from this kind of motivation."

> "...try to set the action steps so they're due right around the time you expect to hold your implementation meetings."

"OK, Mike," said Jerry. "Any other words of wisdom?"

"Yeah," replied Mike. "If you really want to motivate the troops, set several of your most important action steps so that they come due at the same time. Then, announce to your team that, if everyone accomplishes their action steps on time, the next meeting will be held at a really nice venue—back down in the Keys, or in the afternoon at a really nice conference facility followed by a great dinner, a game of golf, etc."

With that, Mike and Jerry talked some more about the three-day meeting they had two weeks ago, the trip home, and the outings the group had gone on the last day of the retreat.

"Did Dave and Chuck see any sharks on their eco-tour?" asked Mike.

"If they did, they didn't say anything about it to me," Jerry replied. "They had a great time, though. On the plane on the way home, Dave mentioned to me that he's thinking about bringing his family down. Both he and his wife have Sea•Doos. Dave was talking about the two of them riding the water bikes all the way from Key Largo to Key West."

"That sounds like a lot of fun," replied Mike. "But it'd be more fun if they trolled a Billy-bait along behind the Sea•Doo."

"Billy bait? What's that?" asked Jerry.

"Oh, it's a popular lure down in the Keys. Good for catching Mahi-mahi, sailfish, tuna, whatever happens to be around on the surface of the water. According to Captain Dick, they work at any speed—so you can troll them effectively even when you're going 20 or 25 miles an hour."

"OK, OK, Mike, I've heard enough about fishing already. Next time, I'm bringing my golf clubs down there!"

"Glad to hear there'll be a next time," said Mike.

"Well," said Jerry, "I have to say that I've never experienced a seminar or a consulting session like the ones we had down there. Neither had my management team. They've been working hard at the action steps we developed in Marathon, and they're eager for this next meeting so they can develop new ones. You really sold them that this system works, Mike."

"Jerry, I spent about 15 years selling myself that it worked before I sold it to you," Mike replied.

"Mike, I've got to run. I'll let you know how the meeting turned out."

"Take care, Jerry. And good luck"

> "You really sold them that this system works, Mike."
> "Jerry, I spent about 15 years selling myself that it worked before I sold it to you," Mike replied.

Chapter 34

A few months later. Jerry, his wife Gina and daughter Jacqueline are relaxing by their pool in the back yard. Jerry and Gina had been talking about Cleveland Electronics and the changes it was undergoing.

Gina remarked, "It seems like things are going very well. Only time will tell, but I seem to discern a lack of the kinds of 'fire drills' that used to occupy your time and energy."

"You're probably right, honey. It's not that the company still doesn't have problems, but it seems like the management team is taking a much larger role in running the company and reacting to all of the 'fires' that I used to have to put out."

"And," continued Gina, "I haven't heard you mention cash flow problems in over a month."

"That's because Dave has been working with a couple of people to bring down our receivables and inventory levels. And he's tweaked the IT system so we all get daily reports on customer payments and invoices that are due for payment. And all of us are working on improving our job tracking systems, which helps workflow so that the things the company does are more efficient—and more profitable."

"Daddy," inquired Jacqueline, "if the company is more profitable, does that mean that **you'll** make more money?"

A smile played with the corners of Gina's mouth. She knew what was coming. For some reason, Jacqueline had become interested in animals over the last couple of weeks, and she had been asking Gina about the possibility of getting some kind of pet(s).

"Why do you ask, honey?" replied Jerry.

"Well, now that the school year is finishing up, I've been thinking about how to occupy my time this summer," replied Jacqueline. "And Mom and I have been thinking that maybe having a pet would help me to learn responsibility and perhaps teach me what it means to care for another living thing."

By this time in his career as a father, Jerry could tell when he was being set up. The words issuing from his daughter's mouth sounded a little like Gina's speech patterns. In other words, mother and daughter had rehearsed.

"What kind of a pet were you thinking about, honey?" Jerry asked.

Jacqueline got the thoughtful, wide-eyed look on her face that she had practiced in front of the mirror in her bedroom last evening. She thought back on the discussions she and her mother and her school friends had been having. Jacqueline had devised a strategy she thought would work. She would start by discussing a few of the pets she didn't particularly want before she talked about the one she wanted.

"I've been thinking about a yellow boa constrictor, Daddy," replied Jacqueline.

His daughter's comment sparked a lively discussion about snakes, lizards, and reptiles in general. Jerry expressed considerable anguish over having things like that in his house. Gina pretended to be open-minded about the whole issue.

After about 15 minutes, Gina asked Jacqueline, "Honey, are there any other kind of animals you may be interested in?"

'Wellll..." replied Jacqueline. "My friend Sally has a couple of birds..."

"What kind of birds?" Jerry asked, now eager to steer the discussion away from scaly crawly things.

"She has two parrots, and they're really neat," replied Jacqueline eagerly. "They talk, sing to each other, and they bond to humans," she continued. "Plus they are just beautiful to look at."

"What do Sally's birds look like?" asked Gina.

"They're both the same kind. Mostly green, with yellow and blue faces. And colorful red and yellow markings on their wings. In fact, I think they're called blue front Amazons," said Jacqueline.

Jerry thought... *"My, my what a coincidence. I wonder what those birds Amber had were called?"*

The family discussed birds some more. They decided to take a trip to a local pet shop that carried birds that weekend, and Jacqueline would buy a bird magazine for Jerry to read. With that, Jerry and Gina got back to their discussion of the company.

"I'm really looking forward to Mike's attending our next implementation meeting tomorrow," remarked Jerry.

"Is this the first time you've seen him since Marathon?" asked Gina.

"Yes. Although, as you know, I've been sending him copies of our Issue/Action Agendas, and he's been coaching me over the telephone."

"Well, then he's well read in on the improvements the company's made," replied Gina.

"Oh, absolutely," said Jerry. "I just can't wait 'til he sees the changes we've made. And by the way, Gina, won't the chlorine in the pool tarnish that silver Cobb coin necklace you're wearing?"

"Honey, if 250 years at the bottom of the ocean didn't hurt this coin, nothing will."

Chapter 35

7:30 AM next morning. Dave Kork's office. Dave and Chuck are discussing the meeting that will start in about 90 minutes with Mike Henderson and the team. Suddenly, Sam Lufkin, the day shift production foreman, knocks on the door and barges into Dave's office.

"Sorry to come barging in like this, Chuck, Dave, but we've got a major problem."

"What?" asked Chuck curtly.

"You know the last shipment of those connectors for Unisonictelcom that are supposed to ship Friday? Well, inbound QC just rejected the shipment of plastic moldings we're going to need to make our deadline. And when our people called the supplier to get parts in here that met spec, they were told that the supplier had no more on hand, and they would have to reorder from China."

"In other words," said Chuck, "we're talking 30 or 45 days."

"At the very least," replied Sam.

The three talked more about the problem and possible solutions for the next half-hour. As Sam left to follow up on several possible corrective actions, Chuck said to Dave,

"We'd better go tell Jerry."

With that, they went to Jerry's office and outlined the problem. Apparently, this particular Unisonictelcom order was so critical that failure to deliver would mean the loss of the account for sure. Towards the end of their discussion, Amy came in.

"Mike's here," she replied.

"Well, have him come in," said Jerry. "We've got a live disaster in the making right here. Let's see if he can solve this one for us."

When Mike came in, they went over the problem and possibilities. The appointed time for their implementation meeting came and went as they discussed the disaster at hand.

"Hey, guys!" exclaimed Mike. "What time was our implementation meeting due to start?"

"Ten minutes ago," said Jerry. "But this problem's critical. We need to see what Sam comes up with so we can make some decisions here. And make them fast."

"While we're waiting for Sam to do his part, why can't we get our meeting going?" said Mike. "We can always break when appropriate to deal with this latest problem."

With that, Amy assembled the rest of the team in the company conference room. Cleveland Electronics' newest member of the team, Dan LaMonical, VP Sales and Marketing, was introduced to Mike.

Jerry opened the meeting: "OK, team, as a special treat today, we're going to have Mike lead the meeting for a change. That way, you can see what I've been doing wrong these past couple of months."

With that, Mike took over as moderator. He first went through the Issue/Action Agenda that Amy had updated as a result of the last meeting two weeks ago.

"Amy, when did this latest agenda go out to everyone?" asked Mike.

"They had it a week ago today," said Amy.

"Excellent" responded Mike. "Now, let's got through our issues, and make sure we have the priority right."

When Mike took the team through this step, he noted that certain priorities had changed, been combined with other issues, and a couple of new items had been added since the meeting down in Marathon. All very normal and expected for a company using the Issue/Action Agenda system in a proper manner. Mike also noted that all action steps had been completed on time.

As they were about to end discussion of Issue #2 and move on, Jerry called for a short break. "I need to find out if Sam's made any progress on our Unisonictelcom problem," he remarked.

"Jerry, I agree you need to find that out, but you need to remember two things," said Mike.

"And those would be?" asked Jerry, obviously irritated.

"Number one, once you start one of these meetings, it's supposed to go for its allotted two hour time limit. Otherwise…"

"Yeah, yeah, I know," said Jerry, now somewhat red in the face. "And what else?"

"And, if you're following the chain of command, Chuck should be the one dealing with the problem, not you," finished Mike.

Chuck interjected "I agree. And I told Sam that he shouldn't interrupt this meeting. In fact, we set a time of ten thirty to go over what he has found out and to decide further action steps."

"Super," said Mike. "Just the way it ought to work. Any problems with that, Jerry?"

"No, I guess not," the President grumbled. "Let's get on with our meeting."

With that, the team finished the Issue/Action Agenda. At the stroke of 10:30, Sam knocked on the conference room door and was invited in. He reported that the vendor had located parts at its production facility in China, and they would air freight the items to Cleveland today. The parts would arrive tomorrow, in time to meet the customer's shipping requirements. Jerry and the managers ended their meeting on a happy note. Jerry and Mike adjourned to Jerry's office, while the rest of the team returned to their individual responsibilities.

Once at ease in Jerry's office, Mike asked, "So, Jerry, how are things really going?"

Jerry replied, "Amazingly well. You saw how most of the action steps we decide upon get done, didn't you?"

"Sure did," replied Mike.

"And, our banker just loves our business and strategic plan that we put together out of our meetings." With that, Jerry pulled a two-inch thick document from his desk drawer and presented it to Mike. The document contained the team's result of the Ten Point Planning Process, everything from mission, vision, and core values to annual and three-year financial plan (budget) and the Issue Action Agenda for the last implementation meeting.

"Jerry, I'm very impressed," said Mike. "And how are your profits and cash flow?"

"Profits are good, Mike," replied Jerry. "Cash flow could be better, but it's taking us a while to get our inventory levels down to where they should be. But that'll improve as we get further along in refining our IT system."

"What about operations in general?" asked Mike. "Do you still have a lot of fire drills of the type we witnessed here this morning?"

"You mean with the parts order?"

"Yes."

"We still have our share of glitches. But, as you saw a little bit ago, more and more of these are being handled by lower level managers and supervisors. It feels like fulfilling a customer order is more of a **business process** than an **event**."

"That's outstanding, Jerry," replied Mike. "So, when do you want me to check in next?"

> "It feels like fulfilling a customer order is more of a *business process* than an *event*."

They discussed this for a few more minutes, and then decided that November 1 would be an appropriate date for a follow up meeting.

"That'll be about the time you'll have a good idea of your year-end results as well," said Mike. "It'll be interesting to see how close to budget you expect to come."

With that, Jerry and Mike bade each other goodbye, and Mike left.

Chapter 36

A couple of months later. Mike Henderson, Jerry and the management team are in the company conference room. They're discussing the numbers David Kork has put up on the white board in front of the room:

	000's $			
	Year before	Last year	This year	Next year
Sales	19,635	22,068	26,035	28,000
Gross profit-$	5,498	5,517	8,132	10,920
-% of sales	28%	25%	31%	39%
Selling, general and admin expenses	4,756	5,267	6,842	8,120
Pre-tax income-$	742	250	1,300	2,800
Pre-tax income-% of sales	4%	1%	5%	10%

"What a difference!" Mike exclaimed. "Tell me, Dave. Did anything we did in Marathon have something to do with this year's results?"

"Well, first of all, Mike," interjected Jerry, "I should point out that our first five months, through May, was showing a loss of $400,000 or about $80,000 a month. So, our operating results for the last seven months of the year showed profits of one point seven million dollars, which is even more remarkable than Dave's numbers show."

"Anyway, Mike, the answer to your question is, 'Definitely yes.' When Chuck and I went over our projections for next year a couple of weeks ago, we made a list of the 'Top Five' profit contributors that came out of what we did in Marathon."

"Excellent, Dave," remarked Mike. "Would you and Chuck mind sharing them with the group?"

"Not at all," said Chuck. "I have the list right here. The first item is big—cut average cycle time on Unisonictelcom orders by eight point five hours, or 12 %."

"And how'd you do that?" asked Mike.

"It's a combination of a lot of things," said Chuck. "But, in short, our people have a better understanding of how to work with our IT system, which results in better data, which results in fewer 'glitches' in the system, better spotting of potential backlogs in the production process, and improved communication among the people and departments the work has to flow through before it ships."

> "But, in short, our people have a better understanding of how to work with our IT system, which results in better data, which results in fewer 'glitches' in the system, better spotting of potential backlogs in the production process, and improved communication among the people and departments the work has to flow through before it ships."

"So, a combination of a better IT system along with better training of the people operating the system?" asked Mike.

"Right," answered Chuck.

"The second biggest item is cost savings on unprofitable work," said Dave. "When we did an Activity Based Cost Analysis on a couple of our suspected 'loser' products, we were very surprised, to say the least."

"What?" questioned Henderson, "The losses turned out not to be losses after all?"

"No, just the opposite," replied Chuck. "We found out that our 'losers'—primarily a couple of types of capacitor sub-assembly configurations we were making for a few of our older customers-were costing us 'way more money than our older costing systems were telling us. So, we discontinued manufacturing these configurations and helped our customers find a new source. We were able to cut three people and free up 3,500 square feet of floor space which we were then able to re-deploy more profitably."

"Good," remarked Mike. "What's next?"

"I'll talk about this one," said Jerry, "since Dave's probably too embarrassed to bring it up."

"Oh, go ahead, Jerry," replied Dave. "I've already braced myself."

"One of our divisions operates a little differently than the rest of the company," explained Jerry. "The division essentially does long-term contract work for the government and a couple of defense contractors. We had suspected for a long time that we were losing a lot of money on the type of contract this division has, but the monthly divisional P & L wasn't showing this. When Dave went over some of the system and procedural changes with the people doing the accounting for that division, we found out that the accounting for that division was using the same accounting method as the rest of the company, which was inappropriate."

"We were recognizing earnings when the contract was billed instead of being on the 'percentage-of-completion method,'" interjected Dave.

"Yeah…well…anyway," continued Jerry, "when Dave got into it, he found out that we were racking up huge losses on this particular type of contract."

"So we stopped taking that kind of work, and results immediately improved," summed up Dave.

"Did anyone assess the dollar amount of that item?" asked Chuck.

Dave replied, "If we would have picked up on the issue a year earlier, we would have saved $350,000."

"Wow," replied Mike. "So, now at least, you'll save $350,000 a year in the future."

"Right," said Dave. "And, although this was an embarrassing experience, it does give me an important new asset."

"What's that, Dave?" asked Henderson.

"The next time someone starts telling me Accounting's not as important as any other part of this company, I'm going to tell this story," replied Dave.

"You're right there," said Jerry. "In fact, I've been thinking about moving Accounting from the trailer out back in the parking lot to those empty offices up front here."

"You mean next to sales?" inquired Amy.

"Yep," Jerry replied.

"I'm having a heart attack!" exclaimed Dave.

With that, everyone had a good laugh, and went back to discussing the rest of the "Top Five" list. When that part of the meeting was over, Amy said, "Mike, would you like to see the results of our new Business Growth Model questionnaire?"

"Sure," replied Mike. "Although I think I already know how it'll come out. When did you folks retake it?"

"Last week," said Jerry. "Amy, why don't you put up that chart we worked on last night."

With that, Amy displayed the following:

	Original	Last week
Phase I	15	12
Phase II	24	14
Phase III	6	18
Phase IV	4	4

"OK," said Mike, "congratulations. I think that chart, and the financial results we just went over, say it all, don't you?"

The group agreed, and expressed their appreciation to Mike for a job well done. Mike thanked the team, and expressed his hope that they'd all be seeing each other again soon. With that, the meeting ended, and Mike and Jerry headed over to Jerry's house for drinks and dinner.

Chapter 37

An hour later. Jerry's house. Mike, Jerry, wife Gina and daughter Jacqueline are admiring Jacqueline's new pet.

"What a pretty bird!" Mike exclaimed. "Does he talk?"

"It's a she, and she doesn't talk yet," replied Jacqueline. "She's just a baby. Four months old today, I think."

"Well, she's certainly very cute," said Mike. "Where'd you get her?"

"Down in the Keys," replied Gina.

"As a matter of fact, Mike, we got her from your friend Amber," Jerry interjected.

"Ah, ha, that's why this little one looks so familiar," replied Mike. "She's one of the brood that Amber's Lo-lo birds had!"

"Right," replied Jerry. "Say, Gina honey, shouldn't dinner be about ready?"

*   *   *

Later that same evening. Mike and Jerry are enjoying after dinner cigars and brandy on the deck overlooking Jerry's huge back yard. Jacqueline had gone to her friend's house, and Gina went to see one of those "art-house" movies that Jerry never cared to see.

"Jerry, it seems like your company's back on track and running well," remarked Mike.

"It is, Mike. Maybe too well."

"Too well?"

"Yeah. Operationally, things are so smooth that sometimes I feel useless. But luckily, just when I think business is getting to be boring and no fun anymore, along comes a new problem or challenge to make life interesting."

"Like the China problem you mentioned in the car this afternoon?" asked Mike.

Companies like Jerry's that manufactured and assembled small electronic components were being increasingly challenged by China's cheap labor. Many of Jerry's customers, large OEM's who went to China a few years ago in hopes of breaking into the huge Chinese market, were now putting pressure on their Tier One and Two suppliers to go over to China and open operations there. In this way, the OEM's were hoping to capture the best of both worlds—cheap Chinese labor, plus the considerable manufacturing efficiency to be gained by dealing with suppliers who understood the OEM's way of doing business and who were already integrated into the OEM's supply chain.

"Jerry, I understand that China's a real challenge for companies like yours today," remarked Mike. "What are you planning to do about it?"

"That's why I wanted us to talk privately, Mike. I've been thinking that if I could find a smaller company already doing business in China, perhaps one that's struggling with low profits so that it doesn't cost a lot of money, perhaps you and I could turn it around and eventually integrate it into Cleveland Electronics' operations."

"What kinds of things would this company be manufacturing?" asked Mike.

"Ideally, it would be assembling components similar to the ones I make into larger sub-assemblies or even finished product," replied Jerry.

"I see," said Mike. "So this new company could in effect be buying from Cleveland Electronics…"

"…and selling to customers in the U. S. and China," finished Jerry.

"And I suppose this new company would also, ideally, be sourcing some of its parts in China?"

"Ideally, yes," replied Jerry. "And, Mike, as a matter of fact, I've been talking to a little company I've had my eye on now for, Oh, maybe four years or so…"

The End

SUPPLEMENTAL IMPLEMENTATION MATERIAL

---

[1] Adapted form a presentation, Evolution of a Business, by Gleeson, Sklar, Sawyers & Cumpata, LLP, 1997

Exhibit A   Evolution of a Business Presentation

Evolution of a Business

 *From start up to professional management and planning*

Successful Navigation of the Business Cycle

1) Danger signs in a company
2) Evolution of a Business
3) Phase I Company
4) Phase II Company
5) Phase III Company
6) Phase IV Company
7) Benefits of becoming a Phase III or Phase IV Company

Ten Danger Signs In Companies

1) Not enough hours in the day.
2) Too much time putting out fires.
3) People not aware of what others are doing.
4) People lack understanding of where company is headed.
5) Owners and executives complain that there are too few managers.
6) Managers have to say, "I have to do it myself if I want it done correctly."

Ten Danger Signs In Companies

7) People feel that meetings are a waste of time.

8) When plans are made, there is inadequate follow up.

9) Some feel insecure about their place in the Company.

10) The company continues to grow in sales but not in profits.

Phase I - Characteristics

- Founders often still there and running the company

- Founders are technical achievers or market builders; usually not strong managers

- Emphasis is on producing products or services and selling them

- Minimal emphasis on management, systems, planning, etc.

Phase I - Characteristics

- Organization and communication informal
- Long work hours – modest salaries
- Management reacts mostly to customers rather than employees
- Growth greater than inflation but moderate

Phase I – Problem Areas

- Not clear who is in charge when there are two or more founders or partners in the business
- Conflicts between founders or partners
- New employees not motivated by dedication
- Poor accounting and cash control

Phase I – Problem Areas

- Working capital shortages
- Minimal financial planning
- Little or no business planning
- Temptation to diversify into unrelated businesses

→ **CRISIS: Leadership and Systems**

Phase I - Management Emphasis

- **ACCOUNTING AND FINANCE:**
  - **Basic accounting and financial control:**
    - **Financial statements**
    - **Operating budget**
    - **Cash flow projection**
  - **Design and implementation of accounting systems**
  - **Cash management**
  - **Build supportive banking relationships**
  - **Personal financial planning**
  - **Financial performance data interpretation**

Phase I - Systems and IT

- Needs determination
- Hardware/software selection
- Implementation planning and conversion

Phase I - Sales and Marketing

- Product mix determination
- Product pricing and break-even analysis
- Build permanent customer base
- New product development or selection
- One-year sales plan

Phase I - Operations

- Basic resource scheduling
- Purchasing and inventory control
- Production (operations) performance reporting
- One-year production plan

Phase I - Management and Leadership

- Owner conflict resolution
- Leader selection
- Determine responsibilities of key jobs

Phase I - Personnel

- Basic benefits
- Basic wage and salary
- Balancing owner compensation with needs of company

Phase I - Business Strategy and Planning

- One-year business plan
- Strategy Emphasis: Survival, Growth and Profitability
- Clarify business niche
- Owner goals versus abilities

Phase I - Business Strategy and Planning

- New product or service strategy
- Growth strategy: Decision to stay in Phase I or become Phase II or III
- Ownership continuity and funding

Phase II - Entrepreneurial Expansion Phase

- CHARACTERISTICS
  - Leader chosen and accepted
  - Often multiple locations, such as: sales and branch offices
  - Detailed attention given to areas in addition of producing products or services and selling

Phase II - Entrepreneurial Expansion Phase

● CHARACTERISTICS

- Employee duties are more specialized, formally defined and communicated
- Company becomes more impersonal
- Growth rate faster than Phase I; sometimes accelerates to a very fast rate

Phase II - Entrepreneurial Expansion Phase

● CHARACTERISTICS

- Employee duties are more specialized, formally defined and communicated
- Company becomes more impersonal
- Growth rate faster than Phase I; sometimes accelerates to a very fast rate

Phase II - *Entrepreneurial Expansion Phase*

▣ PROBLEM AREAS:

- Poor decisions are made in areas such as; information technology, facilities expansion, hiring key employees, use of cash, financing
- Problem solving is time consuming
- Key employees become disenchanted and leave
- Financial performance and control systems are often inadequate for sales volume

Phase II - *Entrepreneurial Expansion Phase*

▣ PROBLEM AREAS:

- Shortages of management time and cash
- Reactionary planning
- Temptation to sustain faster growth so loyal employees will have opportunity
- Temptation to diversify into unrelated business

→ *Crisis - Management Team and Systems*

Phase II - Operations

- Facilities and equipment planning

- Product (operations) control

- Finished goods inventory control

- Cost accounting

- One-year production plan

Phase II - Management and Leadership

- Build an aligned management team
- Turn technicians into managers
- Plan and implement managerial accountability
- Determine responsibilities and expectation of key jobs
- Recruit key personnel
- Broaden external business awareness
- Introduce internal client concept

Phase II - *Personnel*

- Incentive sales compensation
- Management and technical training
- Employee performance evaluation process
- Compliance with government requirements
- One year manpower plan

Phase II - *Business Strategy and Planning*

- One to three-year business plan
- Strategy Emphasis: Growth, Survival and Profitability
- Product or services strategy
- Design action plans as part of business planning
- Goal: Become a Phase III Company

Phase III - Professional Management Phase

◈ CHARACTERISTICS:

▪ **Aligned management team in place (Phase II crisis solved)**

▪ **Necessary financial performance reporting and control systems in place and operational**

▪ **Decentralized organization by function, product/service or location**

▪ **Company has identity beyond the founder(s) and current leader**

Phase III - Professional Management Phase

◈ CHARACTERISTICS (continued):

▪ **Short and intermediate term plans in place**

▪ **Managers doing more managing than technical work**

▪ **All elements critical to success bases are covered**

▪ **Profit centers established**

▪ **Growth rate moderate -- usually slower than Phase II**

Phase III - *Professional Management Phase*

● PROBLEM AREAS:

- **Reaction to change becomes difficult -- reaction time has increased**
- **Senior management feels it is losing control -- less direct contact with day-to-day operations**
- **Increased vulnerability to outside factors, such as:**
  - Government   Competition
  - Unions

Phase III - *Professional Management Phase*

● PROBLEM AREAS:

- Increased vulnerability to internal factors, such as:
  - **Politics**
  - **Outdated corporate culture**
  - **Bureaucracy**

Phase III - Professional Management Phase

● PROBLEM AREAS:

- **New business opportunities continually identified but reaction to them is cumbersome -- trial and error**
- **Threatened by Phase IV competitors**
- **Little communication from the top**

Phase III - Management Emphasis

● Accounting and Finance

- **Management-by-exception reporting systems**
- **Long-range financial plan**
- **Create chief financial officer position or upgraded controller position**
- **Financial data interpretation**
- **Budgetary process**

Phase III - *Management Emphasis*

- SYSTEMS AND IT
  - **Upgrade to meet needs of an expanding company**
  - **Selection of management and technical personnel**
  - **Intermediate range IT planning**

Phase III - *Management Emphasis*

- SALES AND MARKETING
  - **Market share analysis**
  - **Market expansion plan**
  - **Sales forecasting**
  - **One-two year sales plan**

Phase III - Management Emphasis

- OPERATIONS
  - **Production (operations) planning to coordinate with marketing and sales**
  - **Cost reduction (efficiency)**
  - **R&D autonomous from production**
  - **One-two-year production plan**

Phase III - Personnel

- Profit related compensation plans
- Executive compensation planning
- One-two-year manpower plan
- Compliance with government regulations

Phase III - Management and Leadership

- Succession management planning
- Management development
- Managerial accountability

Phase III - Business Strategy and Planning

- One-three-year business plan
- Strategy Emphasis: Profitability, Growth and Survival
- Acquisition and new venture planning

Phase IV- Professional Planning

- ● **CHARACTERISTICS:**
  - **Each product group/business unit is treated as an investment center**
  - **Emphasis on return on invested capital**
  - **Intra-preneurship**
  - **Incentive compensation plans are in place**
  - **Generally cash is not a problem**
  - **Shared commitment**
  - **Consistent performance**
  - **Planning is part of culture**

Phase IV- Professional Planning

- ● CHARACTERISTICS *(continued)*:
  - Oriented to both sales and profits
  - Authority and power coalesce
  - Systems for information and control in place
  - Organization has vitality and momentum

Phase IV- *Professional Planning*

● PROBLEM AREAS:

- **Not enough well trained people**
- **Some in-fighting**
- **Insufficient managerial training**
- **Lower expectations for growth**
- **Rewards those who do what they are told to do**
- **Employees and lower level management suspicious of change**
- **Low internal innovation**
- **Managers still don't have authority equal to responsibility**
- **Bureaucracy**

Phase IV- *Professional Planning*

● CRISIS:

- **Management conflict**
- **Bureaucracy**
- **Systems and procedures dominate behavior**

Phase IV- Management Emphasis

◈ **ACCOUNTING & FINANCE**

▪ Information, budgeting and control systems

▪ Develop role of VP of finance or CFO

▪ Refinement of budgetary process

Phase IV- Management Emphasis

◈ **SYSTEMS & IT**

▪ Emphasis is on centralization at headquarters

▪ Build systems to provide information and control – long term IT plan

▪ Selection of management personnel

Phase IV- Management Emphasis

◈ SALES & MARKETING

- One to three year sales plan based on forecasts
- One to three year marketing plan
- Responsibility dispersed

Phase IV- Management Emphasis

◈ OPERATIONS

- One to three year operations plan
- Responsibility dispersed
- Continuous improvement

Phase IV- Management Emphasis

● PERSONNEL

- Management development training
- Problem solving training
- Team building training
- Executive compensation planning
- Compliance with government regulations

Phase IV- Management Emphasis

● MANAGEMENT & LEADERSHIP

- Succession management planning
- Maintain entrepreneurship
- Management development

Phase IV- Management Emphasis
● BUSINESS STRATEGY & PLANNING

- Develop strategic plan

- Satisfying customer needs

- Care and feeding of employees

- Emphasis on remaining flexible

- Strategy emphasis: profitability and growth

- Acquisition and new venture planning

Benefits of Becoming a Phase III or IV Business

● Survival and continued development of the company are not dependent on one or a few people

● Management succession is more assured

● More capable employees can be hired and retained

Benefits of Becoming a Phase III or IV Business

- Existence of a strong middle management team frees executive management to plan, pursue additional markets and react to major opportunities and problems.

- The company can more effectively expand product lines and markets

Benefits of Becoming a Phase III or IV Business

- **The company is more able to react to an adverse economy or market.**
- **Profitability is usually sustained**
- **The increased flexibility and stability usually makes the business more enjoyable for the owners/managers and key employees, because planning replaces fire fighting**
- **The owners can spend more time away from the business if desired**
- **The business has higher market value**

Exhibit B   Blank Owner/Management Team Assessment

OWNER/MANAGEMENT TEAM ASSESSMENT

Name of Company/Evaluator :

Instructions

Read the questions on each of the attached 4 pages. Score each question according to the following:

2	Very true
1	Somewhat true
0	Not true at all

In other words, is each statement **very true**, **somewhat true**, or **not true** at all of your company?

When you are done, add up the scores for each phase, and write them here:

Summary Evaluation:

Score:

Phase I—Entrepreneurial start up ☐

Phase II—Entrepreneurial expansion ☐

Phase III—Professional management ☐

Phase IV—Professional management and planning ☐

*The growth phase having the highest score indicates the growth phase of your company. If the company also scores high in an adjoining phase, this may indicate that the company is in an **early** or **late** stage of its growth phase. For example, scores of 14,16,8 and 6 in Phases I through IV, respectively, may indicate a late Phase I company.*

The above indicates that we are a(n) (early, middle, late) Phase_____company.

OWNER/MANAGEMENT TEAM ASSESSMENT
Phase I—Entrepreneurial Start-Up

Numerical score
(2, 1 or 0):

☐   Founders are running the company

☐   Founders are technical achievers or market builders-usually not strong managers

☐   Emphasis is on producing products or services and selling them

☐   Minimal emphasis on management, systems, planning, etc.

☐   Informal organization and communication structure

☐   Long work hours-modest salaries

☐   Management reacts mostly to customers rather than employees

☐   Growth rate is greater than inflation, but moderate

☐   Not clear who is in charge when there are two or more partners in the business

☐   Conflicts between founders or partners

☐   New employees not motivated by dedication

☐   Poor accounting and cash control

☐   Working capital shortages

☐   Minimal financial planning

☐   Little or no business planning

☐   Temptation to diversify into unrelated businesses

☐   **Total Phase I score**

OWNER/MANAGEMENT TEAM ASSESSMENT
Phase II—Entrepreneurial Expansion

Numerical score (2, 1 or 0):

☐	Leader chosen and accepted
☐	Often multiple locations, such as: sales, branch offices, warehouses
☐	Detailed attention given to areas in addition to producing products or services and selling
☐	Employee duties are more specialized, formally defined and communicated
☐	Company becomes more impersonal
☐	Growth rate faster than Phase I; sometimes accelerates to a very fast rate
☐	Delegation is increasingly difficult for the leader
☐	Access to the leader becomes difficult
☐	Qualified managers are not permitted to make decisions in their technical areas
☐	Managers are technically oriented and not accustomed to making their own decisions
☐	Poor decisions are made in areas, such as: data processing, facilities expansion, hiring key employees, use of cash, financing
☐	Problem solving is time consuming
☐	Key employees become disenchanted and leave
☐	Financial performance and control systems are often inadequate for sales volume
☐	Shortages of management time and cash
☐	Reactionary planning
☐	Temptation to sustain faster growth so loyal employees will have opportunity
☐	Temptation to diversify into unrelated businesses
☐	**Total Phase II score**

OWNER/MANAGEMENT TEAM ASSESSMENT
Phase III—Professional Management

Numerical score
(2, 1 or 0)

- [ ] Aligned management team in place

- [ ] Necessary financial performance reporting and control systems in place and operational

- [ ] Decentralized organization by function, product/service or location

- [ ] Company has identity beyond the founder(s) and current leader

- [ ] Short and intermediate term plans in place

- [ ] Managers doing more managing than technical work

- [ ] All elements critical to success bases are covered

- [ ] Profit centers established

- [ ] Growth rate moderate

- [ ] Reaction to change becomes difficult-reaction time has increased

- [ ] Senior management feels it is losing control-less contact with day-to-day operations

- [ ] Increased vulnerability to outside factors, such as: government, unions, competition

- [ ] Increased vulnerability to internal factors, such as: politics, outdated corporate culture, bureaucracy

- [ ] Reaction to new business opportunities is cumbersome

- [ ] Threatened by larger competitors

- [ ] Little communication from the top

- [ ] Need for longer range planning is evident, but resistance to doing it

- [ ] Temptation to commence faster growth rate than company can absorb

- [ ] **Total Phase III score**

OWNER/MANAGEMENT TEAM ASSESSMENT
Phase IV-Professional Management and Planning

Numerical score
(2, 1 or 0)

☐ Product groups/business units are treated as investment centers

☐ Emphasis is on return on invested capital

☐ Incentive compensation plans are in place

☐ Generally cash is not a problem

☐ Consistent financial performance is the norm

☐ Planning is formalized and is a part of corporate culture

☐ Company's culture is oriented to both sales and profits

☐ Systems for information and control are in place

☐ Some in-fighting exists among employees and management

☐ Insufficient managerial training is a problem

☐ Company's culture rewards those who do what they are told

☐ Employees and lower management are suspicious of change

☐ Low levels of internal motivation is a problem

☐ Managers do not have authority equal to responsibility

☐ Shortages of well trained people are a problem

☐ Bureaucracy is a problem

☐ Organization has vitality and momentum

☐ **Total Phase IV score**

Exhibit C   Examples of Company Infrastructure

Examples of Company Infrastructure

Employees

—Personnel manual

—Standard personnel action forms

—Employment history form

—Job descriptions

—Written performance evaluations

—Formal employee counseling/goal setting process

Operations

—Machinery utilization reports

—Job scheduling system

—Work center production reports

—Job costing system

—Comparison/follow up system on actual v. estimated costs

—Delivery due date tracking system

—Material/Enterprise requirements planning system

—Daily stock status reports

Organization

—Organization chart

—Written business plan with accountabilities

—Strategic planning base

—Documented succession plans

—Emergency/disaster plans

Sales/marketing

—Sales projection/plan for each rep/office/customer/product line

—Effectiveness measures for advertising campaigns, programs

—Competitive analysis

—Jobs bid/jobs won/jobs lost tracking system

Finance and management

—Monthly financial statements

—Weekly or daily "flash reports"

—Annual/monthly budgets, updated

—Monthly written Management's discussion of operating results

—Five year financial projections

—Five year capital budget

—Comparison of actual v. benchmarks for key financial indicators

Exhibit D   Ten Point Planning Process

Ten Point Planning Process

1) Determine mission/vision/core values/guiding principles

2) Define the business you are in

3) Set growth goals: Phase I, Phase II, Phase III

4) Determine key jobs and get the right people in them. Define the management team.

5) Determine what is needed to get harmony in the management team and/or family

6) Define manager accountability

7) Set financial goals to get a balance among:

   -Profit

   -Cash flow

   -Equity

8) Identify core systems and determine what is needed to make them work

9) Identify industry trends and set product goals (stars and cash cows)

10) Create action plans: Assign responsibilities, budgets and target dates

Exhibit E   Blank Issue/Action Agenda

Key Issue	Discussion	Action Steps	Responsible Person	Due Date	✔ = Complete

0-595-30985-2

www.ingramcontent.com/pod-product-compliance
Lightning Source LLC
Chambersburg PA
CBHW030921180526

45163CB00002B/424